To Gerry Fleet.
with best wishes
from George Barker,
ask me back to London
I really enjoyed meeting
you.

THE BOEHM JOURNEY
TO EGYPT
LAND OF TUTANKHAMUN

by Frank J. Cosentino

Foreword by
MME. ANWAR EL-SADAT

EDWARD MARSHALL BOEHM, INC.
TRENTON, NEW JERSEY 08638 USA

About the Author:
Frank J. Cosentino joined Edward Marshall Boehm, Inc. early in
1959 as executive assistant to Mr. and Mrs. Boehm. In addition to
his involvement in all aspects of the Boehm experience, Mr.
Cosentino travels extensively, presenting lecture programs and
porcelain exhibitions. He is now President of Edward Marshall
Boehm, Inc. and Boehm of Malvern England Ltd.

Mr. Cosentino has also written *Boehm's Birds—The Porcelain Art of
Edward Marshall Boehm,* the biography *Edward Marshall Boehm
1913-1969,* and *The Boehm Journey to Ching-te-Chen, China, Birthplace
of Porcelain,* recounting the historic Boehm trip of 1974 as guests of
the People's Republic of China.

Photography:
Boehm travel photos by Frank J. Cosentino and Maurice Eyeing-
ton. Porcelain still photography by Photographic Illustrations,
Ltd., Philadelphia, Pa.

We gratefully acknowledge the use of the following:
Philae Temple photographs on pp. 96, 101 (B), and 102 (A), cour-
tesy of the Organization of Egyptian Antiquities.
Sphinx at Gizeh on p. 18 and historical figures on p. 20, from the
New York Public Library Picture Collection.

Library of Congress Catalog Card Number: 78-61164
ISBN 0-918096-02-2

Edward Marshall Boehm, Inc., Trenton, New Jersey 08638

To the Boehm artists and craftsmen,
whose expressions in porcelain
help many enjoy
the art of the ages

Contents

Title	Page
Foreword by Mme. Anwar El-Sadat	ix
Introduction	1
The Land and the People	11
Historical Review of Ancient Egypt	21
Old Kingdom	23
First Intermediate Period	27
Middle Kingdom	29
Second Intermediate Period	35
New Kingdom	37
The Decline	59
The Journey to Cairo	61
Abu Simbel	89
Aswan and Philae	97
Luxor and Karnak	107
The Valley of the Kings	119
The Return to Cairo	130
Reflections	133
Bibliography	139
Index	141

Acknowledgments

The author is grateful to the many associates and friends who contributed to this journal: Mrs. Edward Marshall Boehm who invited me to share the trip to Egypt with her and with Maurice Eyeington, head sculptor of our studios; Mme. Anwar el-Sadat for her support of our project and for her contribution of the Foreword; His Excellency Ashraf A. Ghorbal, Ambassador from Egypt to the United States, and Mrs. Ghorbal for involving us in Tutankhamun and for their invitation to visit Egypt as guests of the government; Minister Abd El-Monem El-Sawi for approving our trip under the auspices of the Ministry of Culture of Egypt; Dr. Mohammed Gamal El-Din Mokhtar, President of the Organization of Egyptian Antiquities, and his staff for their guidance, cooperation, and warm hospitality throughout our stay in Egypt; the people of Egypt from all walks of life who extended kindness, friendship, and unusual patience with our many questions; Mr. Thomas Hoving and his staff of the Metropolitan Museum of Art with whom we liaised in developing our porcelain re-creations of Tutankhamun and other selected ancient Egyptian treasures; my staff associates who assisted in the publication of this book; and all of our studio artists and colleagues both in Trenton, New Jersey and Malvern, England who have contributed to building the Boehm Porcelain Experience.

Frank J. Cosentino, President
Edward Marshall Boehm, Inc.

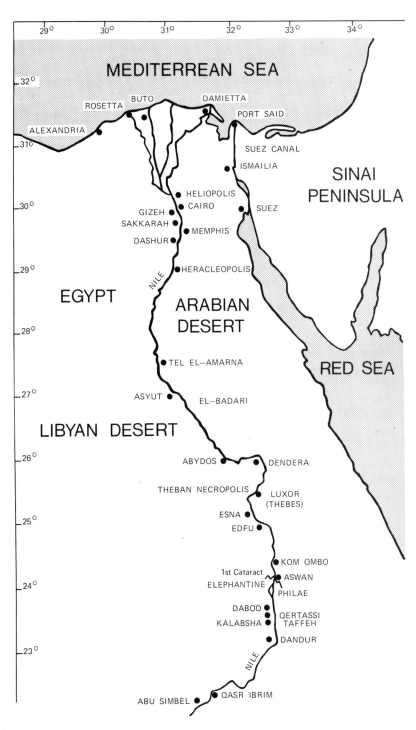

SCALE 1″ = 100 MILES

Mrs. Helen Boehm and Mme. Anwar El-Sadat at Abdine Palace, Cairo.

Foreword
by Mme. Anwar El-Sadat

I am delighted to have been asked to write a Foreword for this book, as I am firmly convinced that people learn to understand one another and to respect one another in the kind of journey described in these pages. What really matters in human encounters is that people should be made aware of each other's interests, ideas and ways of doing things. *The Boehm Journeys* contribute handsomely to this purpose, by bringing home to the host country the genuine human dimension of the American people—kind, hard-working people, with a sense of humour, candour and compassion.

Another precious service rendered by *The Boehm Journeys* is that they also bring back to the English-speaking reader an impression of a country, not inflated or disfigured by propaganda, but simply told through the description of men and women at work and play.

I am confident that my own country, Egypt, will be projecting through these pages an image of warm humanity and affection for the simple rhythms of Nature. We are primarily a nation of peasants, dwelling and working and speculating about the mystery of life on the banks of a generous river. Our qualities and defects are those of all children of the soil: we are peace-loving and devoted to family and home; we can be simple and unsophisticated in our joys and cares, but we can also regard the world with the eyes of long experience and patience in the face of hardships. Patience and reverence of life are seen in our attachment to all we hold most dear. . . our loved ones, our country and the dignity of our people. We are also, like every genuine peasant, clearsighted about the realities of everyday life, and we feel that it is by our own efforts and our own strivings that we shall achieve the fruits of progress and civilization borne by our hard-won independence.

Yet we are not closed in on ourselves. We consider all humanity our brothers and sisters, and we have, from time immemorial, stretched out the hand of friendship to the world beyond our frontiers. At the crossroads of three continents, and on the land which has witnessed the birth of civilization as it is known in the world today, we cannot be comfortable in an atmosphere of prejudice and mutual distrust.

The treasures of our ancient culture, touring the U.S.A. as I write these lines, are a pledge of our declaration of faith in the vocation for peace and friendship which we regard as our birthright.

May this *Boehm Journey* reflect in its readers' hearts some of the infinite funds of good will and international solidarity which are the very foundation of the Egyptian personality.

Jehan Sadat

Jehan El-Sadat
First Lady of Egypt

THE BOEHM JOURNEY
TO EGYPT
LAND OF TUTANKHAMUN

January 31st, 1977

Dear Mrs. Boehm,

As a long standing admirer of Boehm porcelain I would like to say
how impressed I have been with some of the commemorative art objects
portraying aspects of the cultures of different countries.

It occurred to me recently on one of my visits to the"Treasures of
Tutenkhamen" Exhibition that Boehm might be interested in producing
one of their wonderful works of art to commemorate the two years the
exhibition will be in the United States; possibly a figurine, or perhaps
a plate.   I would be only too happy to escort you round the exhibition
should you be interested - it will be in Washington for another six weeks
before moving to Chicago where it opens in mid-April. Also, if my idea
seemed a viable proposition I would be pleased to arrange for you to
pay a visit to Egypt so that you could see other aspects of our culture
first hand.

I look forward to hearing from you.

                    Yours sincerely,

                    Ashraf A. Ghorbal
AAG/vb   Ambassador

p.s. I have just heard from our mutual friend, Tom Hoving, Director of
the Metropolitan Museum, that we have some beautiful birds in Egypt which
might be suitable for your collection of birds.

Introduction

The new year of 1977 had barely turned and we at the Boehm Studios in Trenton, New Jersey, were preparing for the annual introduction of our new porcelain collections.

An art-viewing phenomenon was taking place at the National Gallery in Washington, D. C. The ancient Tutankhamun collection was breaking all attendance records, and overwhelming numbers of people were pressing to see it. Our interest in Tutankhamun was high because of our artistic orientation; but we anticipated no additional involvement other than joining the long lines of admirers in Washington.

Then, on February 2, Mrs. Edward Marshall Boehm received the letter on the opposite page.

This letter had enormous impact on us as we considered and discussed its contents. Re-creations of ancient Egyptian art forms would be a dramatic departure for our studio artists. We at Boehm have long been engaged in the portrayal of natural things, of birds, animals, and flowers. This strong identification with nature was set by our founder, Edward Marshall Boehm, 1913–1969, whose porcelain expressions were an extension of his real vocation as naturalist and animal husbandryman. He will always be remembered for his important work in ornithology and aviculture; but he also bred and showed, with great success, cattle and dogs of various breeds, tropical fish, fancy fowl, and horses.

Edward Boehm accomplished more than fifty first-breedings of exotic bird species; his great Holstein herd was led by one "Arctic Rose" who set the standards for milk and fat production and who was the supreme choice over all dairy breeds for her beauty and conformation; one year his fancy fowl won seven of ten awards in the annual midwestern show; among his dogs was "Rickie," a black and white cocker spaniel who garnered fifty-one first-place ribbons before he was retired; at present, nine years after Mr. Boehm's death, his stables of standardbred pacers and trotters continue to be an important factor in improving the breeding and performances of harness horses.

1

Such a deep-seated involvement with natural life, which extended so easily to the work of the studios, had accumulated energy over the years. The questions we had to confront, therefore, were important to the future direction of our studios. How would this affect our current program of naturalistic sculptures in planning for the next two years? How to turn the skills and attitudes of our artists and craftsmen—a finely-honed team whose total involvement for two and a half decades has been one with nature—toward the re-creation of fine art treasures? And how would patrons and collectors of Boehm porcelains receive such new creative directions? Moreover, would they recognize them as Boehm? Cognizant of the pressure of time, could we, in just a few months, in an intricate hand-creating process which often consumes more than a year to finalize one new sculpture, focus our energies to complete a collection of excellence and importance?

The "safe" response to Ambassador Ghorbal would have been to refuse involvement. But two factors spurred us to a positive reply. We knew the versatility and enormous talents of our team of artists and craftsmen, a group which is second to none in the world of porcelainists; so we were confident of our capabilities to re-create the collection superbly.

Secondly, we succumbed to the lure of the fabled boy-king, Tutankhamun. Who can resist the attraction of the young pharaoh who, more than thirty-three hundred years ago, was crowned King of Egypt, the most powerful and advanced country of his world? Who does not feel a deep sense of compassion and pity for a child who had no childhood and upon whose frail body was placed the enormous scepter of his country? All adults certainly can understand the tragedy of so young a king, especially when they visualize a child of their own placed in similar circumstances.

Tutankhamun affects young people as well, who might have an even greater understanding of him. On the one hand they can dream the dreams of all children of a land of gold and riches, of being a king with powers over heaven and earth and over all living things. Remember, as kids, when someone became "too big for his breeches," we would say, "Who do you think you are, King Tut?" At the same time youngsters can empathize with Tut. They feel his vulnerability as a young king, how frightened and confused he must have been when first seated on his throne watching a parade of other kings, of princes and princesses, of viziers and attendants prostrating themselves before him. "He couldn't just get up like me and go out and play with other children. He couldn't wear comfortable clothes, climb trees and hills and come home torn and dirty from rollicking around. He probably wasn't even allowed to laugh or cry." From their own favorite fables they understand the guile and treachery of some of those around the boy-king who must have been planning his demise, looking to usurp his power and position. The fact that he died at the age of eighteen before the zenith of his manhood, whether naturally or by the hands of others, intensifies this great compassion for Tutankhamun.

Ambassador and Mrs. Ghorbal followed up the letter with an invitation to Mrs. Boehm and the author to have dinner with them and mutual friends at the Embassy residence in Washington, D. C. This was to be preceded by a visit to the Tutankhamun collection at the National Gallery after normal visiting hours. Dr. Ibrahim El-Nawawe, First Curator of the Egyptian Museum in Cairo, personally conducted us on a two-hour tour of the collection, carefully describing each of the treasures. Apart from the empathy for the boy king, which we all shared, we were awed by the beauty and opulence of what we saw. It was difficult to keep one's perspective as to time and place. Only fifty-five art objects were on display, out of about five thousand found in the young pharaoh's tomb, a tomb which is one of the smallest in the Valley of the Kings and which might not have been the most splendid in its riches and art. From the boy-king's possessions and accouterments, one can only begin to assess the remarkable degree of artistry and craftsmanship from one of the great periods of Egyptian art, over thirty-three hundred years ago!

All were excited and stimulated as we enjoyed dinner. Helen Boehm had already formulated in her mind many of the subjects for our studio re-creations in porcelain. In addition to her overseer role as chairman of the Boehm Studios, it is she who conceives the new designs and who serves as catalyst and motivator among the studio artists. She explained to Ambassador and Mrs. Ghorbal that only those treasures which lent themselves to artistic translation into high-fire porcelain should be selected; and that objects other than Tutankhamun, but of the same period, should be considered.

The Ghorbals are gracious, attentive people, Mediterranean in appearance and mannerisms, erudite, and in full command of the English language. They are among the most liked and respected of the foreign diplomatic corps in our nation's capital, and they are good friends of the West. After the discussion of prospective subjects for our porcelains, our hosts suggested that we plan a trip to Egypt, as guests of the government, to see other treasures in the ancient collections, to study, photograph, and sketch in the museums and temples and to enjoy Egypt as it is today. Further, if we were able to schedule a trip the end of May and early June, we would have the added pleasure of attending the forthcoming wedding of the Ghorbals' daughter, Nahed. We accepted the invitations without hesitation.

In the course of the evening Ambassador Ghorbal explained how the tour of Tutankhamun's treasures was arranged and the organizations involved in its sponsorship. The loan originally was agreed to by former Secretary of State Henry A. Kissinger and Egyptian Foreign Minister Ismail Fahmy during the visit of President Nixon to Cairo in June 1974. The first announcement was in a joint communiqué in the final meeting between President Nixon and President Sadat. The formal agreement was signed in October 1975. By mutual consent of all participating sponsors, The Metropolitan Museum of Art was chosen to coordinate and administrate for the consortium of six hosting U. S. museums. Acting for the Egyptian government were the Organization of Antiquities of the Arab Republic of Egypt and the director of the Egyptian Museum in Cairo. A portion of the monies raised through admissions and the sale of re-creations would benefit Egyptian cultural institutions, primarily the Cairo Museum.

Prior to departing from the Egyptian Embassy that early February evening, the Ambassador extended one more invitation. He suggested that our team of artists immediately schedule a trip to Washington and spend ample time with the Tutankhamun treasures. This was arranged within a few days. Our colleagues returned equally enthused and eager for the project. After several meetings, and one week after receipt of Ambassador Ghorbal's letter, our creative team set to work. Other programs were suspended temporarily. Our goal was to complete an initial collection of twelve re-creations by the end of July, less than six months away.

Our creative team reached new artistic heights with Tutankhamun. The zeal and energy with which the artists and craftsmen worked surpassed that of all prior projects including the five-foot-tall "Ivory Woodpeckers" sculpture of 1963, the life-size "Mute Swans" made for China in 1972, and the massive "Eagle of Freedom" completed for our Bicentennial in 1976. Their stimulation was derived in part from the usual dedication to new work and from the opportunity to show their versatile skills. Part of it was due to the overwhelming excellence of the ancient art treasures in the touring collection. How much of it could have been attributed to the mesmerizing effect of the boy-king's face as reflected in the magnificent effigy mask, the disarming, guileless look of a gentle youth, burdened by his royalty, staring at them across thirty-three centuries?

The selection of subjects for re-creations in porcelain represented a cross section of the materials and forms of the Eighteenth and Nineteenth Egyptian Dynasties (1567–1195 B.C.). Those marked with an asterisk (*) are not from the tomb.

The Great Gold Mask of Tutankhamun, which covered the mummy's head. Of beaten and burnished gold, it is studded with inlays of lapis lazuli, faience, quartz, carnelian, colored glass, obsidian and green feldspar. The plaited false beard is ceremonial. Vulture and cobra heads symbolize the king's sovereignty over Upper and Lower Egypt.

Cheetah Head. A symbol of motherhood. The head-post of one of the animal-sided funerary beds. Made of stuccoed and gilded wood, the nose and drops under the eyes are inlaid with blue glass, the eyelids with black glass.

Hathor, the Sacred Cowhead. Goddess of many feminine functions and attributes. Made of wood, the face and ears are gilded. Graceful horns and neck are plated with bronze leaf and varnished black. The eyes are of crystalline limestone and obsidian, lined with black glass.

Anubis, the jackal-god, aide to Osiris in the netherworld. Made of wood and varnished black. Body details are gilded except for the claws, which are silver, and the eyes which are of obsidian and alabaster.

* *Horus,* the falcon deity and sky-god, identified with the pharaohs during their lifetimes. It is of gold with obsidian eyes. The crown is with stylized plumes and a cobra, symbols of divinity and sovereignty.

Golden Throne Panel. A magnificent scene on the inner back panel of the boy-king's gold throne features Tutankhamun and his queen, Ankhesenamun. Their forms are of glazed terra cotta; headdresses are turquoise-colored faience; robes are of silver. Other details are inlaid with colored glass, carnelian, calcite, faience and translucent stone. Gold overlays all uncolored portions of the scene.

Ivory Chest Lid. The top of the ivory-inlaid wooden chest, this is one of the most important works of art found in Tutankhamun's tomb. The scene of the king and queen is carved into the lid. Ivory inlays are shaded with stains of off-white, rose, ochre, silver, and a variety of blues.

Faience Cup. One of the keys which led to Howard Carter's discovery of Tutankhamun's tomb in 1922. Several years earlier it had been unearthed in the Valley of the Kings by another excavator. It bears Tutankhamun's engraved cartouche on its side. Egyptian faience was made of ground quartz and glass, with colors added, which were fused and molded into shapes, primarily utilitarian vessels. It is different from the heavily glazed earthenwares of the West called faience (or delftware, or majolica).

Cartouche. A wooden cartouche-shaped box probably used on ceremonial occasions. It bears Tutankhamun's name in ebony and painted ivory hieroglyphs in relief against a gilded background. Its symbolic shape represents the king's rule over all that the sun encircled.

Scarab. Symbolic of creation and of the rising eastern sun. Found on many objects in the tomb. In the cartouche-shaped box was a magnificent scarab bracelet encrusted with lapis lazuli and with a decorative border of gold, lapis, turquoise, quartz, and carnelian.

Bird In Nest. An alabaster jar cover which depicts a primitive bird, newly-hatched, among four eggs in a nest. The eggs and bowl are of alabaster, the bird is carved of wood, painted and stuccoed, and has an ivory tongue.

* *Lotus.* Official flower of Upper Egypt. Each morning the pharaoh, equated with the sun-god, was born from a blue lotus floating on the receding waters of the great primordial ocean.

Selket. Goddess of childbirth, nursing, and magic. In the tomb she was found with her three goddess-sisters protecting the canopic chest of Tutankhamun. Carved of wood, overlaid with gesso and gilded.

* *Bastet.* Cat-goddess, a symbol of motherhood and of a woman's love and joy. Carved of wood, varnished black, with painted eyes, a gold necklace and one gold earring.

Perfume Bottles. A joined pair in the form of cartouches made of gold and attached to a silver pedestal. Bas reliefs within the cartouches are of Tutankhamun as a young boy. Inlays are of polychrome glass, lapis, turquoise, red jasper, calcite, and carnelian.

Tomb Guardians. Two life-size statues of the king, with black skin, stood at the door of his burial chamber. Black, the color of Egypt's rich soil, was associated with Osiris and regeneration. Made of wood, varnished black and embellished with gold.

Falcon Emblems. Another depiction of Horus. Mounted on golden standards with flails on their backs and collarettes with counterpoises. Gold leaf over wood.

* *Ibis.* Sacred symbol of the god Thoth, god of science, culture and wisdom. The body is carved of wood and gessoed, the beak is bronze.

Child King. A realistic sculptural portrait of Tutankhamun as a young boy being born from a blue lotus. A beautifully detailed bust carved in wood and overlaid with painted gesso. Eyebrows and eyelashes are blue in imitation of lapis, of which the sun-god's hair was believed to be made.

Votive Shield. One of eight shields found in the tomb. Of incised and gilded wood, it depicts Tutankhamun brandishing a scimitar in one hand, while in the other he is holding aloft by their tails two lions which symbolize his enemies.

Ceremonial Chair Panel. Carved inner back panel of one of Tutankhamun's chairs. Incised and carved of a wood reddish in color, probably cedar. The god of eternity, Heh, is the dominant figure with inscriptions of Tutankhamun's name and of his divine origin.

* *Obelisks.* Pyramidal spires of stone reaching in tribute to the sun-god. Usually carved in granite and in pairs. The tips were veneered in gold or electrum to reflect the sun and to mirror its color.

Harpoonist. Tutankhamun on a boat of papyrus stems hunting the dreaded hippopotamus, symbol of Seth, god of evil. Wood-carving gessoed and gilded, with eyes of obsidian.

Shawabty. "He who answers on behalf of another." One of 413 miniature figures placed in the tomb to serve the king in the next world. Carved of cedar in the likeness of Tutankhamun. Bears the crook and flail, emblems of the power of Osiris, god of the dead.

Alabaster Mask. One of four stoppers from the top of a canopic chest, the repository for the king's precious organs. In the image of Tutankhamun. Alabaster with painted facial features.

The forms of these antiquities posed no special problems for re-creations into high-fire porcelain. In fact they are relatively simple in comparison with the elaborate naturalistic sculptures for which the Boehm Studios are known. The challenges, apart from the usual complexities of working with porcelain, lay in researching the colors, enamels, and fluxes necessary to replicate the precious and semi-precious stones of the antiquities, and in developing the purest type of gold needed to emulate the beaten, burnished gold of the ancient treasures. An enormous amount of creative energy and research were necessary before our art team was satisfied that we had the materials and techniques required for excellent renderings in fine porcelain.

Starting in mid-February, the sculptural forms rapidly began to take shape among a team of five sculptors led by our head artist, Maurice Eyeington. The initial references were from the ancient objects in the collection at the National Gallery and from the use of outstanding photographs and book references supplied by the Organization of Egyptian Antiquities.

Our final sources lay in the museums in Cairo and Luxor where we would seek out the subjects that were not part of the traveling collection here in the United States. Our trip plans were made. We would depart for Egypt May 27 and would return June 8.

Before proceeding with an account of our fascinating trip to "the land of Tutankhamun," it is important that we briefly review the land and the ancient history of its people. For the reader interested in studying Egypt in depth, an impressive number of books have been written by historians, archaeologists and Egyptologists, some of which are contained in the bibliography of this report. This review is intended merely as a stagesetting so the reader may better enjoy the purposes of our project, the significance of the Tutankhamun collection and of other Egyptian antiquities, and Egypt as it is today.

Mrs. Boehm with Ambassador and Mrs. Ashraf A. Ghorbal. The Boehm porcelain re-creations were unveiled at the Egyptian Embassy, Washington, D.C., July 25, 1977, Egypt's National Day.

At Karnak Temples, Ahmed Abd El-Rady (right), our Antiquities Organization host in Luxor, with a temple guard.

The Land and the People

The long history of Egypt is difficult to comprehend. Only recently we in the United States celebrated the Bicentennial of our country; and we can all recall our school years and the volumes we waded through trying to understand the origins of our people, the development of our land, and the chronology of historical events. We think of the glories of ancient Greece just a few centuries before the beginning of Christian time, and of the Great Roman Empire which followed, and then faded, sixteen hundred years ago. In 1974, during a journey which we took through China, we were awed by our trip to Ching-te-Chen, an ancient Chinese city in which the secrets of porcelain-making first were unlocked shortly after the birth of Christ; and we admired and understood the art, technology and organization of the great Chinese Dynasties which terminated with the collapse of the Ching in 1911.

Yet these civilizations are relatively recent compared to the history of Egypt. To the ancient Greeks, Romans, and Chinese the civilization of Egypt was even more ancient, for it pre-dated them more than their civilizations have pre-dated us! Ancient Egypt began to rise over six thousand years ago and it burst into a full glory and power that was to last for approximately twenty-seven hundred years. Mention of the peoples of southern Europe appear in Egyptian writings for the first time about 1300 B.C., a period during which the power of the pharaohs already was beginning to decline. The earliest fixed date in the history of man is 4241 B.C. when the Egyptians conceived the first 365-day calendar, a thirty-day month and a twelve-month year. A cohesive political and social structure began to develop at the end of the Predynastic Age, approximately 3400 B.C. Hieroglyphic writing, centralized rule, and the coordination of trade skills, agriculture, art and architecture quickly evolved and flourished under a long succession of kings.

The title of this chapter, "The Land and the People," encapsules the elements which set ancient Egypt apart from other early civilizations and which help explain its early rise as a nation of political prominence and cultural excellence. The geography of the land—its location and superb climate, the life-giving waters of the great Nile River, rich natural resources, and unique isolation from outside influences—is perhaps the primary contributant to its rapid evolution as a great empire and to its long continuity over so many centuries. The fiber of the people, of course, hardy, intelligent, and industrious, is the second factor. No matter how great the power and influence of the pharaohs, had it not been for the character of the workers and peasants, much less would have been accomplished. For from this vast proletariat came the farmers, masons, carpenters, minor artisans, and construction workers.

The eastern Mediterranean and surrounding regions just to the east and south formed the cradle of man's civilization. Six to ten thousand years ago roving bands of primitive people began to merge and to form loose communities in the valleys of the Tigris, Euphrates, and Nile rivers. Civilization in Mesopotamia might have progressed simultaneously with that of Egypt, had the river valleys a similar geography; but the people of the Tigris-Euphrates lived on an open plain, at the crossroads of the western Orient, unprotected by natural barriers. They devoted much of their time to defending themselves and to rebuilding their war-ravaged possessions. Egypt, however, was well-insulated from outside forces. On the east and west lie two virtually impassable desert wastelands; to the south are the unnavigable rapids (cataracts) of the upper (southern) Nile; and on the north the meandering, harborless Nile branches flow through the Delta and into the Mediterranean Sea.

It was only at the northeast and northwest corners of the Delta that mobility in and out of the Nile Valley was practical, apart from a slight movement of adventurers through the southern cataract region. The racial makeup of northern and southern Egypt reflects these corridors of access. The northern Egyptians combine the characteristics of the Semitic populations of western Asia with the Mediterranean-European influence of the Libyan races. As one travels south up the Nile, the Negro characteristics of the northern Sudan become increasingly dominant.

The Nile below Egypt is formed primarily by two major tributaries which meet just north of Khartoum, the White Nile which has its origin in the equatorial lakes of Africa, and the Blue Nile which gushes forth from the mountains of Abyssinia. From this juncture the Nile flows north another thirteen hundred miles before it reaches the Mediterranean. In southern Egypt, the land of Nubia, hard sandstone has forced the river into a torturous course forming irregular channels and cataracts. Above Aswan the river enters softer limestone beds and thereafter runs a much easier and straighter course north across the eastern edge of the Sahara.

The valley formed by the Nile varies in width up to about thirty miles. Its flood plain was covered with rich alluvium annually brought down from the tropical rains and melting mountain snows south of Egypt. As the river nears the Mediterranean it enters the Delta area formed by silt deposited over thousands of years. The Delta measures about one hundred miles south to north and is a rich, cultivable area.

In effect, the narrow Nile Valley is an oasis in the North African deserts, a thin green belt running south to north through Egypt, a distance of approximately seven hundred fifty miles. Its slow-moving, navigable waters allowed commerce to develop easily. New supplies of rich loam were deposited from June to November, replenishing the soil for agriculture. In time canals and irrigation systems were built to better control the flood waters and to extend the annual growing season.

The climate of Egypt is almost always predictable. It is practically a rainless land below the Delta. From north to south in winter, climates range between 40°F and 70°F; in summer from 90°F to 125°F. But the air is dry and not oppressive as in other parts of the Middle East, and the nights are cool.

This fertile, comfortable land was a veritable breadbasket for its people. Papyrus, lotus, and palms grew in profusion, as did pastures to support large herds of cattle and other domestic animals. It served as a conduit for raw materials and supplies moving north and south. The surrounding deserts provided building materials, minerals, rich deposits of gold, and precious and semiprecious stones. Fish were prolific in the Nile and hunters had a plentiful range of wild animals and birds.

It is no wonder that the wandering tribes outside Egypt yearned to be part of her. They heard tales of this land of plenty and some made their way through the natural barriers in search of a better life. The steady trickle of immigrants was not enough to upset the tranquillity of the valley, and newcomers were comfortably assimilated into the population.

The sameness of climate, the ever-present river, the ribbon of green truncated on the east and on the west by the harsh desert hills, and the relative isolation added up to a somewhat placid, strictly ordered life for the early Egyptian. His natural environment was predictable and clearly defined and he knew of little beyond what he could see. Like other early societies, he looked at these phenomena as the powers which ruled his mind and life, as his gods. The river, earth, sun, sky, hills, trees, birds, animals and sea life were different from him and had qualities or capabilities he did not possess, and all were seen as important influences and forces. Those which benefited him he looked upon as good gods; those which imperiled him were considered bad.

Some early Nile dwellers saw the sky in the form of a gigantic cow, with its head in the west and its hind parts in the east. It carried on its broad stomach the stars and moon, and the sun was born of her every morning as a young calf. In other widely separated villages they saw, instead, a female figure in the sky, bending over in an inverted "u" shape from east to west; and the sun was born every morning as a child. The newborn sun rose from the ground in the east, so they equated it with the beetle, the scarab, which also comes out of the ground each morning. Further, although it may die and its soft parts deteriorate, the shell of the beetle petrifies and endures, remains perpetual, like the sun.

The young falcon, not yet strong enough to fly high, personified the qualities of the eastern morning sun. As an adult, highest of all flying creatures, the falcon symbolized the sun at its zenith during the day. A celestial barque, or ship, carried the sun across the heavens on a sea in the sky. As it faded into the west, the weakening sun changed from a falcon into an old man ready for his grave, ready to sink below the ground again.

At night the sun continued its circular trip through the netherworld bringing its light and benefits to the dead, then would rise again in the east the next morning. The manner of passage underground was by a subterranean stream which connected with the Nile. As with the sun, the people believed the Nile made a similar "great circle," spewing forth from the ground at the First Cataract in the south, flowing north and then returning underground where it emptied into the northern sea, the Mediterranean.

The early Egyptians believed it was from Nu, the god of the primeval waste of darkness and chaos, that Atum, the sun-god, was born. He produced another god, Shu, and a goddess, Tefnut. Shu represented the atmosphere, Tefnut the great ocean. From them, two deities were born. Keb, the earth, takes the form of a man lying face-down in the water and upon whose back all things would grow and man and animals would live. Nut, a goddess, became the sky. Keb and Nut bore four deities, two gods and two goddesses. Osiris, the good son, would become king of the dead. Seth, his evil brother, was destined to be the god of storms and violence. Isis, who married her brother, Osiris, became goddess of motherhood and protector of children. Nephthys, the other sister, represented the goddess of women. These nine gods created from Nu formed the divine Ennead which, in later times, was considered one composite, divine being.

Osiris and Isis had a son, Horus. Seth slew Osiris and, fearful of her son's demise as well, Isis protected Horus and raised him in secret. Isis mourned Osiris's death and buried the body, which angered Seth. He unearthed the body, cut it into pieces, and flung them to the far corners of the world. The distraught Isis, using all of her goddess powers, searched until she found the parts and, with the help of Anubis, embalmed and mummified them. Isis then breathed life back into Osiris; but, having been dead, Osiris no longer could be a king on earth. He thence became king of the dead in the netherworld.

When Horus was old enough, he fought and defeated Seth, thereby avenging his father's death. He assumed the throne of his father and became the falcon-headed deity, the sun-god, called by the name Re-Harakhty. Seth, who was not killed, continued his satanic ways.

Some of these "original" gods continued to be honored throughout the early history of Egypt. Others declined in importance as time passed. Each important center had its own local versions and as the centers of population drew close and were eventually unified under the pharaohs, the gods became commingled in a network of confusion. But the sun-god always reigned supreme. He was variously called Atum, Re, Amun, and Aten.

As was discussed before, many gods assumed the form of birds and animals. The sun-god was recognized as a falcon, ram or beetle. Thoth was identified with both the ibis and baboon. Nut was represented as a cow, cat, lion, leopard or cheetah. Keb was equated with a goose. Seth appeared as a pig, okapi, hippopotamus, or an ass. Sobek, a crocodile god, was a netherworld demon. Buto was the cobra goddess important to northern Egypt. Nekhbet was the vulture goddess of southern Egypt. (Shown together, as on the forehead of Tutankhamun's gold effigy mask, these two symbols represent sovereignty over the whole of Egypt.) Bes, a dwarf deity with leonine features, was a protector against terror and the god of childbirth.

Other important gods which assumed human forms are Hapy, god of the Nile at flood-time; Khons, son of Amun and his wife, Mut; Maat, goddess of truth; Neith, goddess-sister of Isis, Nephthys and Selket; and Ptah, patron god of craftsmen.

Around their gods the Egyptians built temples and holy shrines. As the nation unified and the pharaohs grew more powerful, it was natural that they should assume the same divine characteristics of the gods. It was the pharaoh who dedicated the temples and made the offerings to the gods. In return, the pharaoh was given universal ownership over all things and all peoples. He was omnipotent and omniscient. It was he who caused the sun to rise each day, the Nile to flow, all things to grow. He had power over life and death.

The pharaohs developed an elaborate body of priests to carry on the sacerdotal duties of the temples and they evolved an elite class of scribes, educated ministers, to coordinate the widespread villages and towns, collect annual taxes, organize agriculture, conscript for the army when necessary, settle disputes, punish or reward, gather the workers and farmers together for massive construction projects, and carry on all other functions essential to the business of state. These ministerial scribes appointed other literate assistants as the state developed until there was established an elite class, a highly organized bureaucracy of priests and administrators.

With this centralized power and organization, the political and social structure of Egypt crystallized. Needed manpower could be mobilized quickly and efficiently for the building of canals, irrigation systems, palaces and monuments. Most of the population remained in agriculture as its main work, but increasing numbers were drafted and trained as tradesmen, craftsmen and artists.

As the nation became more productive, the seemingly endless material gifts of the Nile brought increasing wealth to Egypt and an over-production which allowed expanded trade with neighboring countries. A fleet of maritime vessels soon was carrying agricultural products, papyrus, handicrafts, gold, alabaster, and other domestic products to the eastern Mediterranean states, down the Red Sea and south to Nubia. Flowing into Egypt were rare woods like cedar and ebony, ivory, silver, lapis lazuli, bronze, copper, turquoise, spices, and animal skins. As commerce increased, new materials, styles and skills poured into Egypt from eastern Asia and northern Africa, further diversifying and enriching the civilization.

With the progress of the nation, the temples and monuments grew even more ambitious, religious rites and ceremonies became more complex, and the provision for the dead became the dominant concern. The Egyptians were the first in the recorded history of man to believe in life in the hereafter. They believed that the body had a vital force, a spirit called the "Ka," which lived forever and that the physical body protected by another spirit called the "Ba" accompanied it wherever it went, even after death. In addition, every person possessed a soul which could assume the outward appearance of a tree, flower, bird, animal, of any visible feature of the landscape or of life. This doctrine of body, spirit and soul carried through to Christianity and, with varying emphases, to other contemporary religions.

The world of the dead was in the west, of course, where the sun-god descended into his grave each evening; so it naturally followed that cemeteries and tombs were placed on the west bank of the Nile at the edge of the Sahara. The vindication of Osiris in the defeat of his evil brother Seth by Osiris's good son Horus was the strong ethical force in the religion. It was believed that one who lived a good life would be welcomed after death by Osiris, king of the dead, and would be restored to life in the hereafter by him.

An elaborate system of mortuary practices evolved as the Egyptians sought better, more foolproof ways to preserve the body for the after-life and to be certain that it was not violated in its resting place. The pharaoh, representing on earth the divinity of the sun-god, Horus, and in death the embodiment of Osiris, received the most elaborate burial and tomb. So great was the belief in the divine powers of the pharaoh that the entire nation was involved in the activity of preparing giant memorials and a monumental sepulchre that was supposedly inviolate for all time.

These preparations for the royal dead spurred the development of building skills and techniques early in the history of Egypt. Organizations of administrators and armies of workers and craftsmen were brought together to plan, locate and build the mortuary temples and tombs. Large endowments were set aside to care for and protect these divine structures even long after burial. With the pharaoh were buried all of his favorite possessions and enough food and supplies to assure him of an equally comfortable life in the world beyond.

The world has never seen anything comparable to these massive stone structures. The great pyramids and the sphinx at Gizeh,

Great Sphinx, Gizeh. (N.Y. Public Library Picture Collection)

Looking across the Nile near the Aswan quarries.

built almost three millennia before Christ, were just the beginning of a building surge which was to last almost two thousand years and which resulted in countless monuments of stone along the entire length of the Nile Valley. The strength and size of the structures contributed to their perpetuity through the centuries, but the conservatism of the people and the climate were important factors. Even through the occasional periods of foreign intrusion, the people tenaciously held on to their religious beliefs and protected their sacred buildings. As to the climate, the lack of moisture slowed decay and deterioration, and the moving sands of the deserts blanketed abandoned cities and structures, thereby preserving them indefinitely.

The Nile also has played an important role in preserving the ancient glory of Egypt. Its annual deposits of silt during flood stages gradually covered uninhabited areas within range of its waters. It is not a great exaggeration to say that one can dig almost anywhere along the valley of the Nile and be rewarded with archaeological discoveries.

Rameses II, 19th Dynasty

Queen Tiye (above) and Queen Hatshepsut (opposite), 18th Dynasty.

(N.Y. Public Library Picture Collection)

Faience Cup by Boehm. The original cup which inspired this porcelain re-creation was discovered in 1907. Bearing the young king's name, it was a vital key to the discovery of the tomb.

The Great Gold Mask of Tutankhamun by Boehm. This remarkable mask, of beaten and burnished gold, was placed over the mummy. It was inlaid with lapis lazuli, faience, quartz, carnelian, colored glass, obsidian, and green feldspar.

Tomb Guardians by Boehm. Two life-size statues of the king stood at the door of his burial chamber. They were made of wood, varnished black, and embellished with gold. Black, the color of Egypt's rich soil, was associated with Osiris and regeneration.

Perfume Bottles by Boehm. This joined pair of perfume bottles, made of gold and attached to a silver pedestal, contained bas reliefs of Tutankhamun as a young boy within its cartouche designs. Inlays were of polychrome glass, lapis, turquoise, red jasper, calcite, and carnelian.

Child King by Boehm. This was a sculptural portrayal of Tutankhamun as a young boy being born from a lotus. The bust was carved in wood and overlaid with painted gesso.

God Anubis by Boehm. The jackal-god Anubis was an aide to Osiris in the netherworld. He reclined upon a shrine before the entrance to the Treasury, guarding the "secret things." The original was made of wood, varnished black; body details were gilded except for the claws, which were silver.

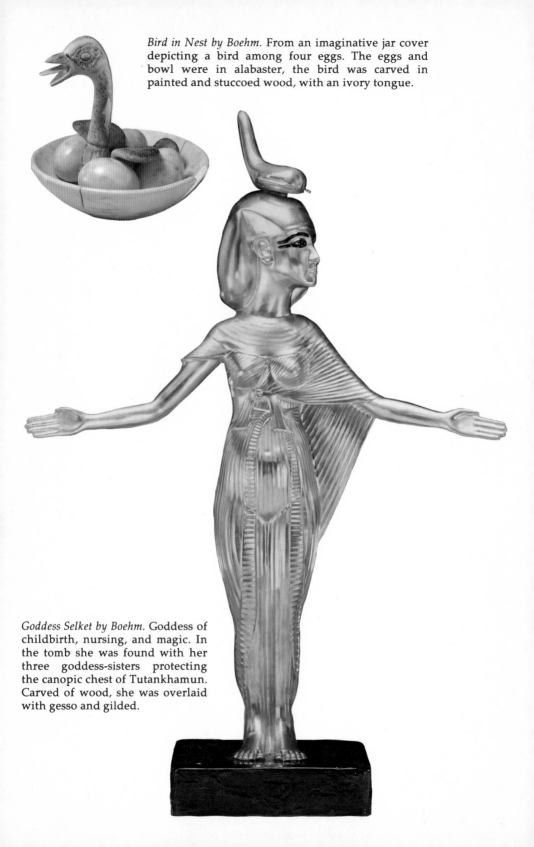

Bird in Nest by Boehm. From an imaginative jar cover depicting a bird among four eggs. The eggs and bowl were in alabaster, the bird was carved in painted and stuccoed wood, with an ivory tongue.

Goddess Selket by Boehm. Goddess of childbirth, nursing, and magic. In the tomb she was found with her three goddess-sisters protecting the canopic chest of Tutankhamun. Carved of wood, she was overlaid with gesso and gilded.

Historical Review of Ancient Egypt

The classification of ancient Egypt into epochs generally follows that of an ancient Egyptian historian, Manetho, who wrote a history of his country in the Greek language around 300 B.C. The work does not exist now but enough books had derived from it to piece together the history as Manetho presented it. Although modern students of Egyptology give little credence to Manetho because of his unscientific tendency to dwell on folklore, his dynastic divisions and nomenclature are used as the standard for Egyptian history. His time standards continue to be refined as the science of Egyptology advances. None can claim to be totally accurate. The subdivision of epochs is approximately as follows:

4241 B.C. .... Introduction of the calendar
Pre 3400 B.C. .... Predynastic Age
3400–3100 B.C. .... The accession of Menes, Unification
           of Egypt
3100–2686 B.C. .... First two Dynasties, Early Dynastic Period
2686–2181 B.C. .... Third through Sixth Dynasties, The
           Old Kingdom
2181–2133 B.C. .... Seventh through Tenth Dynasties,
           First Intermediate Period
2133–1633 B.C. .... Eleventh through Thirteenth
           Dynasties, The Middle Kingdom
1633–1567 B.C. .... Fourteenth through Seventeenth
           Dynasties, Second Intermediate Period
1567–1080 B.C. .... Eighteenth through Twentieth
           Dynasties, New Kingdom
1080–663 B.C. .... Twenty-first through Twenty-fifth
           Dynasties, The Decadence and
           the Rule by Tanite-Amonites;
           Libyans; Ethiopians and Assyrians
663–525 B.C. .... Twenty-sixth Dynasty, The Restoration
525–332 B.C. .... Twenty-seventh through Thirtieth
           Dynasties, Persian Conquest
332–30 B.C. .... Ptolemaic Period, Alexander the Great

The fact that the early Egyptians of the Predynastic Age had a calendar based on the lunar month and solar year is proof enough that their society was remarkably advanced by the fourth millennium before Christ. Little evidence of this society remains other than artifacts of various kinds, but they were skilled in the fabrication of pottery, jewelry, implements, weapons, and utilitarian art forms. They had already formed into small communities along the Nile engaged primarily in agriculture, hunting and fishing; and they had learned the ways of boat-making which indicates that some commerce between villages probably had started.

The concentration of communities developed largely in the northern Delta area and in the south above the First Cataract. Each area came under the rule of various early kings whose coats of arms and symbols were to carry through the history of the nation. Lower Egypt, also called the Northern Kingdom of the Delta, was identified with the papyrus plant, the color red and a serpent-goddess called Buto. Upper Egypt adopted the lotus as its official plant, white as its ceremonial color, and the vulture-goddess Nekhbet as its symbolic deity. Horus was the all-powerful god of both Egypts and their kings.

In time a king would come forth with enough power and organizational strength to unite the two Egypts. This was done around 3100 B.C. by King Menes of the Southern Kingdom. Menes established his royal city at Memphis between Upper and Lower Egypt and began a succession of pharaohs who were to keep the land unified and strong for the next several centuries. Menes and the kings who followed wore the crowns of both Egypts alternately. Eventually, a variety of combinations of the symbols were worn on a single crown through all of the dynasties which followed.

We have seen that a calendar had been fully developed in the Predynastic Period. A form of hieroglyphic writing also was evolving. In the Early Dynastic Period, which covered approximately the First and Second Dynasties (3100–2686 B.C.), the Egyptians had communal agriculture and construction, copper tools and weapons, a thriving commerce by sea, fully developed mines and quarries, sophisticated canal and irrigation systems, rudimentary medicine, surgery, astrology, mathematics, hydraulics, surveying, and all of the basic sciences.

OLD KINGDOM

With the continuing consolidation of power, the kings of the Old Kingdom (Third to Sixth Dynasties, 2686–2181 B.C.) became more and more exalted until they achieved ultimate power; they became synonymous with an all-powerful god and commanded a reverence and respect rarely achieved in the annals of man. The god-king was supreme and the entire life of the nation revolved around him. All worked to please him, to provide him with great riches and comforts; and the first priority of the nation was to build for the pharaoh a great temple and tomb, an eternal house for his life after death.

One of the first and most prominent kings of the Third Dynasty was Djoser (Zoser) who, with the help of a powerful minister named Imhotep, consolidated the supremacy of Memphis and the kings to follow. Djoser apparently recognized the brilliance of Imhotep and wisely allowed him to conduct the temporal, mundane matters of administration while he, the king, maintained a lofty, deific presence. Imhotep functioned as chief scribe, high priest, magistrate and prime minister. So notable were his achievements that he was forever to be remembered in Egyptian history as the god of medicine and the patron spirit of scribes.

It was Imhotep who began the building of temples and monuments on a massive scale. The crowning achievement was the first pyramid built for Djoser, a terraced structure located at Sakkarah. It is constructed of six rectangular stone platforms built on top of each other, the area of each decreasing in size vertically. Up to this time, the traditional tomb was a flat rectangular structure of sun-dried bricks called a "mastaba." Imhotep's creation marked the transition to stone and the pyramidal shape.

The kings of the Third Dynasty which followed Djoser continued to construct larger tombs. A group of pyramids was erected at Dashur. The largest was built by Sneferu, the last and perhaps the most powerful of the Memphite kings. The terraced steps were now filled in to make smooth-sided structures in true pyramidal form.

The pharaohs of the Fourth Dynasty concentrated increasingly more of the nation's labor and wealth on the massive tombs. The original goal of building an indestructible, impenetrable resting place for the body of a king seemed secondary. A king's strength and importance now bore a direct relationship to the size and magnificence of his tomb. Three pyramids were built at Gizeh, the largest ever: the "Great Pyramid," under the direction of Khufu (Cheops), first monarch of the dynasty; the other two built by the kings Khafre (Chephren) and Menkaure (Mycerinus). The Great Sphinx, in the shadows of the pyramids, was believed carved in the image of Khafre.

It is estimated that Khufu's pyramid required ten to twenty years to complete and an army of men numbering as many as 100,000. Two million three hundred thousand hand-carved blocks weighing an average of two and a half tons comprise the structure. Most of the blocks are of limestone, but those used to seal the vault and entrance of the sepulchre are of cut granite.

The quarries were on the east bank of the Nile River just south of Cairo. Here a team freed the stones from the limestone and granite hills. Using copper drills and sand, they pierced holes along lines of intended fracture. Fires were built to expand the rock and the swollen holes were filled with wooden pegs. Then cold water was used to cool the rock and cause it to split away from the pegs. Another team cut away at the blocks with chisels, saws, and hammers of copper and dolorite. Blocks made ready were stored on the east bank until annual flood time when they were loaded on barges and floated across the river to the base of the rising pyramid.

Inclined, step-like terraces were built forming rising ramps around the building site. Using wooden sledges and rollers, each block was pulled by teams and set into place. The remarkable skill and sophistication of the engineers and architects is attested to by the accuracy of this massive mountain of stone. Measuring approximately 481 feet high and 750 feet wide each side, the margins of error of the pyramid's uniform walls are within fractions of an inch. Such incredible precision was accomplished solely with the naked eye and taut leveling strings tied on uniform poles rising from water trenches.

Nine pyramids in all were built at Gizeh. The third largest, built by Menkaure, is small in comparison to the Great Pyramid of Khufu and the second largest of Khafre. The other six are yet smaller than Menkaure's and composed of cheaper materials. Granite blocks were not used and the outer facings were accom-

plished with sun-dried bricks. This decline in quality and monu-
mentality probably was caused by two factors—first, economic
and political problems which gradually would lead to the disin-
tegration of the Old Kingdom. The tremendous resources consumed in building the larger pyramids must have depleted the
wealth of the nation leaving less and less for the ensuing monarchs
to draw from. Second, the increasing power and influence of the
growing body of priests and administrators had begun to dilute
the absolute autocracy of the pharaohs.

Nobles who served as district governors began to consolidate
their support. The high priests continued to develop a national
religion, increasing their numbers and effectiveness as temples
and monuments rose in Upper and Lower Egypt. By the end of
the Fourth Dynasty a subtle shift away from the full equation of
god and king was occurring. To this point the pharaoh and Horus
were one and the same. Now the priests had succeeded in attach-
ing to them the title "Son of Re." In time Re would become the
all-powerful god and the succeeding pharaohs would embody the
sons of Re, an important diminution in the godlike status of the
kings. The cult of Re, represented by the temple priests, was to
remain the dominant religious force throughout the subsequent
centuries of ancient Egypt.

Decentralization of government power followed the same
course. Whereas the first son of a king had been the chief officer
of the state, other chief viziers now influenced weak kings and
their positions became entrenched by a new system of hereditary
succession. The kings of the Fifth Dynasty continued to lose
power until the local governors and priests eventually eliminated
all royal restraints and began setting up their own city states. By
the end of the twenty-fourth century B.C., there occurred a complete dissolution of the nation into separate independent nomes,
or provinces, and the individual ruling families even started
claiming royal status. The kings did not lose all control. They still
had the power of conferring titles and fiefdoms and they still
were accorded the respect due the sons of Re. In addition, they
held the power of the treasury.

The kings of the Sixth Dynasty were not able to re-consolidate
the nation, but through organizational wisdom and force of character they kept the nomes in line. They expanded the official class
and appointed governors and administrators who were fiercely
loyal to the crown. These loyal adherents were richly rewarded for

looking after the interests of the kings. Teti II, Pepi I and Pepi II were particularly effective, and under their control the nation again was able to concentrate its attentions on economic and political progress. Expeditions went south into Nubia and dominated the Negro tribes well below the First Cataract. The army was bolstered by conscripted Negroes and was sent north and east to subdue the troublesome, raiding Bedouin tribes. The river at the First Cataract was cleared of boulders, thus opening a door to the Sudan and Punt and allowing for the increased importation of myrrh, gold, ebony, ivory, ostrich feathers, animal skins, and a host of other materials not obtainable in Egypt. Trade also increased dramatically to the north in the eastern Mediterranean.

The Old Kingdom especially reached its zenith under Pepi II, its last great pharaoh. Pepi II was an organizational genius and a great politician. Under him the boundless energies of the Egyptian peoples were released and properly channeled. His long and uninterrupted reign facilitated this. He ascended the throne when he was approximately six years of age and apparently ruled until he was one hundred, the longest reign yet in the history of man.

When Pepi II died, the remaining years of the Sixth Dynasty were numbered. A few kings followed in the royal line. The rapid decline of the nation is testimony to their weakness, and history has not even seen to it that their names were recorded and remembered. Centralized rule ceased; district governors reasserted their independence and autonomy; petty jealousies and conflicts between nomes quickly developed; organization and mobilization of the masses for agriculture, construction, and commerce slowed; outside forces became bolder in their forays and incursions into Egypt. The Old Kingdom went into decay and Egypt was to enter its "First Intermediate Period," a confusing, nonprogressive feudal age that was to last from the Seventh to the Tenth Dynasties, a time span of approximately one and a half centuries.

FIRST INTERMEDIATE PERIOD

Little is known of the First Intermediate Period (2181–2133 B.C.). It was a time of destruction rather than construction. The nobles of the various nomes zealously guarded their possessions and territories. In an attempt to quickly erase the former power and influence of the great Old Kingdom pharaohs, the mortuary temples and tombs were desecrated and many were torn down. Only the strongest, most monumental structures weathered the devestation.

There was some joint rule in various parts of Egypt as small groups of nomes banded together for preservation. The Memphite families continued to survive through the Seventh and Eighth Dynasties but their influence was increasingly circumscribed. So weak and disorganized were the centers of rule that no monuments of the period remain, if indeed any were built.

The great center of Memphis lost its royal house with the advent of the Ninth Dynasty. Families of nomarchs from Heracleopolis, a city about fifty miles south of Memphis, took the crown and attempted to restore the cult of Horus. Order was restored for a short period of time in the middle of Egypt and there were a couple of generations of peace and new prosperity; but the Heracleopolitan kings and princes also were feeble and their rule would be short-lived.

In the meantime another family of nomarchs was rising in the south at Thebes, approximately 450 miles below Memphis, a city located in a broad, fertile stretch of the Nile Valley just north of the First Cataract. The families Inyotef and Mentuhotpe gradually gained supremacy and broke away from rule under Heracleopolis. A long period of conflict ensued and initially the Theban upstarts were defused. But they gained strength as they consolidated the towns and cities in the south and eventually they prevailed over Heracleopolis. About the middle of the twenty-first century B.C., marking the beginning of the Eleventh Dynasty, power shifted entirely to the south, to Thebes. The Mentuhotpes completed the accession and ruled for five generations, then were followed by an equally vigorous Theban line, the Ammenemes.

Although they had gained their assistance and loyalty in the battle with the north, the new Theban princes were not able to dislodge the powerful southern nomarchs. By this time in history many of them represented long lines of independent sovereigns whose roots could be traced back to the Old Kingdom. They claimed their own brand of royalty and some of their ancestors even had the temerity to challenge the rule of earlier pharaohs. Some were so powerful that they oriented the calendar and dated events by their years of birth and reign; and their lives, in a modest sense, were patterned after the examples set by the pharaohs. They built their temples and monuments, had their own armies and fleets, and accumulated substantial power and wealth.

The Ammenemes could not suppress these independent sovereigns. To attempt to do so would mean the destruction of the south and there was no guarantee of success. They had to accept the situation as it was. The nomarchs were willing to accept some organization into an overall state because they knew it was essential to the future progress and protection of the south; but they would not give up their sovereignty. The situation thus was one of a feudal state whose success was dependent upon the existence of a strong, central monarchy. Any weakness in the central authority would herald a rapid dissolution of the loosely organized city-states. To secure their positions the kings had to surround themselves with administrators of certain loyalty, generally younger men who had grown up in or near the king's households. They were sent into the various provinces as royal governors and commissioners. Each of these crown representatives, in turn, recruited military and scribal attendants and built royal garrisons in the nomes and in the Nubian and Punt frontiers.

MIDDLE KINGDOM

A characteristic of the Middle Kingdom (2133–1633 B.C.) was the evolution of a large middle class. Like the king, the various nomarchs built their own aristocracy of scribes, literary attendants, poets, artists, craftsmen, and militarists. Sons now were following the careers of their fathers in the professions and trades and a stratification of Egyptian society developed. On the highest rungs of prestige and office were the scribes and the literate administrators. Lowest were the peasants, a large toiling class used for agriculture, construction, and when needed, as militiamen.

A re-dedication to the sun-god Re returned in the Middle Kingdom. It had carried through from the Old Kingdom and the First Intermediate Period, but the focus often was blurred through the convulsive dynasties; and many of the more powerful priests and families in the nomes, in their assertions of independence, had selected other gods. Thebes itself had a local god called Amun (Amen, Amon), an invisible spirit which was believed to animate all living things. It now was changed to Amun-Re. As the political fortunes of Thebes rose, so did Amun-Re. It would remain as a mighty religious force through Egyptian history.

Osiris also returned triumphantly and his center of worship was established at Abydos, north of Thebes. The priests determined that Osiris had been buried at Abydos and they gradually developed elaborate annual rituals to the god, turning the city into a holy center. Egyptians of all classes made frequent pilgrimages to the holy sepulchre and all yearned to be buried in the cemeteries near Osiris. Mortuary practices naturally became more complex and the judgment of Osiris, the victory of good over evil, led to a new ethical standard. Osiris became the judge, as well as the god, of the dead, and forty-two demons were appointed as assistants. The deceased was to appear before the judgment panel to profess his innocence of the most common sins of man. His heart then was compared in weight to that of an ostrich feather, the symbol of truth, in order to test the deceased's honesty. Thus, about two millennia before Christ, the Egyptians already had established the religious concept that a good life on earth would guarantee a continuing life after death. Those who did not pass the judgment were condemned to darkness and their bodies to possible dismemberment by a frightening array of netherworld demons.

29

The priests proceeded to devise elaborate guidelines for ethical behavior along with magical formulas, amulets, charms, incantations, litanies, rites, hymns, and words of power to help fortify and protect one from his eventual meeting with the demons and judges of the dead. With such powerful canons, the priests were to gain increasing influence in Egypt and their numbers grew. *The Book of the Dead* was to embody all of the literature and texts of the priests, and its importance can be compared to contemporary bibles. One of the most complete translations is from the "Papyrus of Ani," a body of texts written in the Temples of Thebes and Abydos. The "Ani" was the high officer or chancellor who managed all ecclesiastical revenues and endowments. The following prayers are extracted from *The Book of the Dead*:

The Doctrine of Eternal Life
Hail to thee, O my father Osiris, I have come and I have embalmed this my flesh so that my body may not decay. I am whole, even as my father Khepera [beetle] was whole, who is to me the type of that which passeth not away. Come then, O Form, and give breath unto me, O lord of breath, O thou who art greater than thy compeers. Stablish thou me, and form thou me, O thou who art lord of the grave. Grant thou to me to endure forever, even as thou didst grant unto thy father Temu [the evening Sun-god] to endure; and his body neither passed away nor decayed. I have not done that which is hateful unto thee, nay, I have spoken that which thy Ka loveth; repulse thou me not, and cast thou me not behind thee, O Temu, to decay, even as thou doest unto every god and unto every goddess and unto every beast and creeping thing which perisheth when his soul hath gone forth from him after his death, and which falleth in pieces after his decay.... Homage to thee, O my father Osiris, thy flesh suffered no decay, there were no worms in thee, thou didst not crumble away, thou didst not wither away, thou didst not become corruption and worms; and I myself am Khepera, I shall possess my flesh forever and ever, I shall not decay, I shall not crumble away, I shall not wither away, I shall not become corruption.[1]

Protection of the Heart
Hail, ye who steal and crush heart-cases (and who make the heart of a man to go through its transformations according to his deeds: let not what he hath done harm him before you). Homage to you, O ye Lords of Eternity, ye masters of everlastingness, take ye not this heart of Osiris Ani into your fingers, and this heart-case, and cause ye not things of evil to spring up against it, because this heart belongeth to the Osiris Ani, and this heart-case belongeth to him of the great names, the mighty one, whose words are his members. He

[1]E. A. Wallis Budge, trans., *The Book of the Dead*, p. 70. Copyright © 1960 by University Books. Published by arrangement with Lyle Stuart.

sendeth his heart to rule his body, and his heart is renewed before the gods. The heart of the Osiris Ani, whose word is truth, is to him; and he hath gained the mastery over it. He hath not said what he hath done (?) He hath obtained power over his own members. His heart obeyeth him, he is the lord thereof, it is in his body, and it shall never fall away therefrom. . . .[2]

The Great Judgment
The Osiris Nu, whose word is truth, saith: Homage to thee, O Great God, Lord of Maati [Truth]! I have come unto thee, O my Lord, and I have brought myself hither that I may behold thy beauties. I know thee, I know thy name, I know the names of the Forty-two Gods who live with thee in this Hall of Maati, who live by keeping ward over sinners, and who feed upon their blood on the day when the consciences of men are reckoned up in the presence of the god Un-Nefer [Osiris in his role as Judge]. In truth thy name is "Rehti-Merti-Nebti-Maati" [the two women, the two eyes, the two ladies of Truth]. In truth I have come unto thee, I have brought Maati (Truth) to thee. I have done away sin for thee. I have not committed sins against men. I have not opposed my family and kinsfolk. I have not acted fraudulently (or, deceitfully) in the Seat of Truth [the judgment hall]. I have not known men who were of no account. I have not wrought evil. I have not made it to be the first (consideration daily that unnecessary) work should be done for me. I have not brought forward my name for dignities. I have not (attempted) to direct servants (I have not belittled God). I have not defrauded the humble man of his property. I have not done what the gods abominate. I have not vilified a slave to his master. I have not inflicted pain. I have not caused anyone to go hungry. I have not made any man to weep. I have not committed murder. I have not given the order for murder to be committed. I have not caused calamities to befall men and women. I have not plundered the offerings in the temples. I have not defrauded the gods of their cake-offerings. I have not carried off the *fenkhu* cakes (offered to) the Spirits. I have not committed fornication (or, had intercourse with men). I have not masturbated (in the sanctuaries of the god of my city). I have not diminished from the bushel. I have not filched (land from my neighbour's estate and) added it to my own acre. I have not encroached upon the fields (of others). I have not added to the weights of the scales. I have not depressed the pointer of the balance. I have not carried away the milk from the mouths of children. I have not driven the cattle away from their pastures. I have not snared the geese in the goose-pens of the gods. I have not caught fish with bait made of the bodies of the same kind of fish. I have not stopped water when it should flow. I have not made a cutting in a canal of running water. I have not extinguished a fire (or, lamp) when it should burn. I have not violated the times (of offering) the chosen

[2]Ibid., pp. 451–2.

meat offerings. I have not driven away the cattle on the estates of the gods. I have not turned back the god (or, God) at his appearances. I am pure. I am pure. I am pure. I am pure. My pure offerings are the pure offerings of that great Benu (phoenix?) which dwelleth in Hensu [the metropolis of the twentieth nome of Upper Egypt]. For behold, I am the nose of Neb-nefu (i.e., the lord of the air), who giveth sustenance unto all mankind, on the day of the filling of the Utchat [the day of the full moon] in Anu [the capital of the thirteenth nome of Lower Egypt, ancient city of the sun], in the second month of the season Pert [the late growing season, November to March], on the last day of the month, (in the presence of the Lord of this earth). I have seen the filling of the Utchat in Anu, therefore let not calamity befall me in this land, or in this hall of Maati, because I know the names of the gods who are therein, (and who are the followers of the Great God).[3]

The Ammenemes were skillful and vigorous pharaohs. To protect their flanks when away from the center of power on expeditions north and south, they introduced a practice of co-regency, appointment of the first son to equal position. This strengthened their rule during the Twelfth Dynasty and was to result in nearly two hundred years of progress and prosperity in the Middle Kingdom. After Ammenemes I, the procedure of the royal house was to name the succeeding sons, alternately, Sesostris. Ammenemes I was followed by Sesostris I, he by Ammenemes II, he by Sesostris II, and so on.

The Twelfth Dynasty kings extended their control of the Nile for one thousand miles south from the Mediterranean by again clearing the channel at the First Cataract and setting up garrisons just beyond the Second Cataract. The conquest of Nubia was completed, as were the lands and waters to the Red Sea. Successful military expeditions were carried on to the north in Palestine and lower Syria and the whole of the eastern Mediterranean again flourished in trade. The pharaohs of this period set high standards of achievement for those to follow in later dynasties. They gained reputations as heroic military commanders and through their courage and exploits were able to retain firm control of the nomes and their ruling governors.

Organization of agriculture was raised to an unprecedented level through massive projects of irrigation and the building of canals. Agronomy became a science. A system of measuring annual flood levels, thereby allowing estimates of each year's har-

[3]Ibid., pp. 572–6.

vest, was established by developing the nilometer, a graduated scale on the stone banks of the Second Cataract where minimum and maximum water levels were studied and recorded from year to year. Large natural depressions in the desert adjacent to the Nile were connected with channels so flood waters might be captured and stored in giant reservoirs.

Temples and monuments were built in all cities from the Delta south; and small pyramids, structurally and economically sensible, were built in the area of Dashur, below Memphis. With the exception of the pyramids, most of the structures were unfortunately brought down when later pharaohs like Rameses ii were looking for readily available building materials for their self-styled colossi.

Arts and crafts flourished during the Twelfth Dynasty and portrait painting was developed for the first time. One of the most important accomplishments of the dynasty was the production of magnificent jewelry which utilized precious metals and materials brought into Egypt through increased trade. Some of the finest jewelry the world ever has seen was created during this period. Along with the arts, literature developed and spelling, word construction, and punctuation were standardized. The result was a profusion of treatises on history, religion, the royal houses, scientific and intellectual disciplines, poetry, and drama. The Twelfth Dynasty was truly a classic age. The following is one of the earliest known examples of poetry, written in honor of Sesostris iii during the king's lifetime:

> Twice great is the king of his city, above a million arms: as for other
> rulers of men, they are but common folk.
> Twice great is the king of his city: he is as it were a dyke, damming
> the stream in its water flood.
> Twice great is the king of his city: he is as it were a cool lodge,
> letting every man repose unto full daylight.
> Twice great is the king of his city: he is as it were a bulwark, with
> walls built of sharp stones of Kesem.
> Twice great is the king of his city: he is as it were a place of refuge,
> excluding the marauder.
> Twice great is the king of his city: he is as it were an asylum,
> shielding the terrified from his foe.
> Twice great is the king of his city: he is as it were a shade, the cool
> vegetation of the flood in the season of harvest.
> Twice great is the king of his city: he is as it were a corner warm and
> dry in time of winter.

Twice great is the king of his city: he is as it were a rock barring the
blast in time of tempest.
Twice great is the king of his city: he is as it were Sekhmet [wife of
Ptah, ancient great god of Memphis] to foes who tread upon his
boundary.[4]

The Thirteenth Dynasty, which began about the end of the
eighteenth century B.C. and ended early in the sixteenth century
B.C., was marked by a long list of weak and ineffectual rulers. On
the death of Ammenemes III, perhaps the strongest of the Middle
Kingdom pharaohs, the royal line quickly waned. Predictably, the
feudal state again dissolved. Provincial governors and lords began
to contest each other for power and influence and the nation fell
into bits and pieces, each ruled by a petty kingdom. One pre-
tender after another marched to the throne, some of whose reigns
lasted only a matter of months. In this period of approximately
one hundred and fifty years, record remnants indicate a succession of well over one hundred different monarchs.

Nubia again broke away, as did other occupied protectorates of
Egypt. Trade, agriculture, construction, the arts, and social progress came to a halt. Economically and politically the country degen-
erated. It was only a question of time before strong external forces
would begin to probe once-mighty Egypt and eventually be bold
enough to invade her.

[4]James Henry Breasted, *A History of Egypt*, p. 270.

SECOND INTERMEDIATE PERIOD

During the Thirteenth Dynasty a force from the area of Palestine and Syria attacked and conquered northern Egypt. These people, probably Syrians who ruled the eastern Mediterranean, were called Hyksos. It is not known how long the Hyksos ruled northern and middle Egypt. Some historians estimate as long as sixty-six years, from the Fourteenth through the Seventeenth Dynasties (1633–1567 B.C.). There are varied assessments as to the extent of destruction and exploitation practiced by the conquerers. Building inscriptions show that the foreigners enjoyed being Egyptianized and even adopted the pharaonic styles and titles. No doubt conventional progress remained inert, but the civilization seems to have held together. In fact, the regime at Thebes in the south retained a large measure of independence as the Hyksos were able to extend their rule only to a point about midway between Memphis and Thebes.

The influence upon Egypt was profound and, in some ways, beneficial during this Second Intermediate Period. To this point the Egyptians had a rudimentary approach to warfare, relying on large numbers of conscripted soldiers and militiamen who fought nearly naked and on foot while carrying cumbersome shields. Their weapons consisted of various spears, swords and axes. The Hyksos introduced horse-drawn chariots to the Nile, sophisticated armaments of bronze, the long bow, and the concept of massive warfare with disciplined cadres of charioteers and infantry.

New wool fabrics and techniques of spinning and weaving other than linens were brought from Asia. Bronze was particularly important as copper had been the only basic metal used by the Egyptians in their utilitarian wares. Cultural characteristics of the Hyksos which appealed to the Egyptians were adopted by them. In particular they were attracted to their musical instruments, the tamborine, oboe, and lyre. In retrospect, the experience of the Hyksos domination probably served Egypt well. It filled a power vacuum and was preferable to the alternative of continuously warring feudal lords. Nevertheless the Egyptians despised their conquerers and looked to the day when another strong leader would emerge and expel them.

At the end of the sixteenth century B.C., kings of Thebes, whose predecessors had successfully held the Hyksos back for almost a century, organized the nomes and the people of the south into a strong force. Using the weapons and warring techniques learned from the Hyksos, they began to launch attacks northward toward Memphis.

The glory of liberating Egypt fell to Amosis I (1570–1546 B.C.), first king of the Eighteenth Dynasty. His reign ushered in the New Kingdom, a period of unparalleled progress and power which was to last almost five hundred years, from 1567 B.C. to 1080 B.C. This epoch, which also is called the Empire period, encompasses the Eighteenth through the Twentieth Dynasties.

NEW KINGDOM

Like the Middle Kingdom pharaohs, Amosis I had a genius for politics and organization. He gained the allegiance of the few friendly feudal lords by assisting them when they were confronted with military incursions from Nubia in the south. Unfriendly lords who opposed Amosis or who refused to support the war of liberation were dealt with forcefully and brutally by the king, who often paused in his war with the Hyksos to defeat or punish rival nomes. This is one of the reasons it took so long to expel the Syrians, a period estimated to be more than twenty years. Finally, after years of siege upon Avaris, Delta stronghold of the Hyksos, they were dislodged and began their retreat to lower Palestine.

Amosis I, now a great hero of Egypt, was in a position to eliminate the feudal system, and he did. He confiscated the lands and properties of the lords he defeated and stripped them of their peerage. Those who supported him during the long Hyksos war also turned their estates over to the pharaoh in return for retention of their old titles and offices. All of Egypt once again was the personal property of the pharaoh.

The new state was to take a form different from those of prior dynasties. The king had regained the titular and godlike power of some of the monarchs of the Old Kingdom and the Middle Kingdom, but his more important functions now were as chief of state and supreme commander of the armies. Through the war with the Hyksos Egypt had developed a mighty fighting force and now maintained two formidable divisions, one in the Delta and one in the south. The new aspiration of young men of the middle and noble classes was a professional army career. This standing army had to be maintained and its fighting skills honed. Egypt became a military state and would remain so for the next one hundred fifty years. The army also was a guarantee of the pharaoh's absolute rule. No internal or external opposition would seriously threaten that rule.

Administrative functions demanded much of the pharaoh's time. A new bureaucracy had to be developed to organize the nation. Two viziers were appointed, one for the north and one for the south. The country was divided into sections or districts and each needed a governor as top administrator. This broke down further into cities and towns with key rulers. Separate branches of government were spawned to administer to the treasury and judiciary, and to the agricultural, industrial, and social orders. The multitudinous offices all required educated scribes and recorders. Annual goals were set for agriculture, livestock, construction, and for all goods and services; and tax assessments based on these projections were levied by the treasury. A new body of law developed parallel with the new structure. Justice no longer could be meted out arbitrarily. To establish new ethical guidelines, law had to be precise, understood and consistently equitable.

The ancient institution of the priesthood again flourished; and as they increased in numbers and activity, they became a powerful influence in the New Kingdom. Riches poured into Egypt from foreign conquest and trade allowing the pharaohs to build the most lavish temples and sanctuaries the world has ever seen. The High Priest of Amun, whose offices were in the state temple at Thebes, was head of the nation's religious order. Thousands of temple officials were appointed to administer sacerdotal duties.

Mortuary practices became equally elaborate. Royal burials in mastabas and pyramids gave way to entombment on the west bank of the Nile. *The Book of the Dead* grew as the magic formulae were expanded to further protect the dead in the after-life. Rank and power of royal and noble families were reflected in the size and depth of their tombs and in the possessions and provisions laid to rest with them.

Magical amulets took many forms. To assume the burdens of work and worry in the netherworld, small statues representing peasants and servants of different skills were placed in the hypogeums, or underground tombs. These "Ushebtis" (Shawabtys, Ushabtis) numbered in the hundreds, sometimes in the thousands, in pharaonic burials. The scarab, or sacred beetle, was given even greater importance in protecting the heart from the judgments of Osiris and his demons. When laid on the chest of the mummy it had the power to silence the heart and to prevent it from exposing the evils carried by the heart to the grave. This concept of absolution and the guarantee of a happy after-life has carried through to contemporary religions in the form of sacramental rites.

Eventually mortuary devices subverted ethical codes and conduct. Priests used them for personal gain and influence. Those who could afford the services and the magic of the priests no longer needed to worry about their conduct during life. The wealthier they were, the more vicious and sinful they could be. Any exemptions could be purchased from the priests.

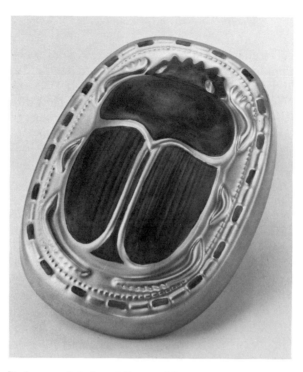

Boehm porcelain Scarab Paperweight.

Amosis I had continued his military campaigns in the north and south, but the greater part of his reign had been devoted to the expulsion of the Hyksos and reorganization of the state. The expansion of the empire was carried forward vigorously by his son, Amenophis I (1546–1526 B.C.) , and by the son's successor, Thutmosis I (1526–1508 B.C.), who appeared to come from another line of the royal house. Through the sixteenth century B.C. the Egyptian armies completed the conquest of Nubia, between the First and Second Cataracts and of the country of Kush, between the Second and Fourth Cataracts. The armies then turned their attentions north, to Syria and Palestine, where a number of small feudal states existed. Strongest was the kingdom of Kadesh, still ruled by the Hyksos. The ethnic fabric of these small states included Semites, Hittites, Mitannis, Hapiru, and Iranians. After many invasions and battles over a period of half a century, Thutmosis I finally extended the empire into the valleys of the Euphrates, Tigris, and Orontes Rivers. Governors and garrisons were established in the conquered lands and soon new tributes and wealth were pouring into Egypt annually.

The marriage practices of the royal families became increasingly complex. For the populace there were laws against incestuous relationships, but as they could with all laws, royalty transcended these and intermarriage was prevalent. They did so to further separate and insulate themselves from their subjects and to keep undiluted their divine powers and essences. The kings had harems but also were prone to marry their sisters and even their daughters. Eldest sons and daughters sometimes married. Further complicating the royal genealogies, polygamous monarchs included the daughters of foreign kings among their wives. This practice further enhanced their sovereignty over vassal states.

The primary loyalty of the pharaohs continued to be to Thebes and its God, Amun, who directed and sustained them in their warring struggles. They showed their gratitude to Amun by lavishing treasures upon him and the lesser gods, and each king tried to exceed his predecessors in the magnitude and opulence of the temples and monuments they built. Sandstone, granite, and quartzite were selected for their strength and durability even though, as a Bronze Age people, their tools and equipment still were somewhat primitive. Gold, silver, and electrum gilded temple walls and fittings. Lapis from Babylon, cedar from Lebanon, and ivory and ebony from Nubia were used in profusion. Thutmosis I gave special impetus to the temple building program. He instructed his brilliant architect Ineni to erect massive pylons (towered gateways) at the entrance to the Amun temple at Karnak and two giant granite obelisks before the pylons.

Thutmosis I had four children with his chief queen, only one of which lived beyond childhood, a girl named Hatshepsut. Among other children with lesser queens was a son named Thutmosis II who married his half-sister, Hatshepsut. The two could produce no immediate heirs but Thutmosis II fathered a son, Thutmosis III, with a concubine from his harem. The father, now king, named his young son as co-regent. Thutmosis II died soon after and Thutmosis III, still a child, ascended to the throne. Hatshepsut, however, had great ambitions. At first she ruled in the name of the young king; but with guile and skill she gained support from the chief viziers, nobles, commanders, and priests, thrust Thutmosis III into the background, and claimed co-regency by right of her birth.

Gradually Thutmosis III was ignored and Hatshepsut became Egypt's greatest queen. Proof of her cunning and strength was her ability to subjugate a man of Thutmosis III's stature for more than two decades; for when he would later regain the throne from his aging aunt and stepmother, he would become one of Egypt's most important kings. Hatshepsut donned both the royal regalia of kingship and a masculine appearance. She wore the double crown of sovereignty over Upper and Lower Egypt and the traditional false beard of the pharaohs.

As a female, Hatshepsut was not interested in carrying on the wars of her fathers. She understood that her place in history could be assured only by building great monuments and works of art. During her rule she turned the nation's attentions to peaceful pursuits. Apart from an insatiable desire for the riches to be drawn from her foreign states, she showed little interest in their conduct and political stability. Under the direction of her father's old architect, Ineni, and her favorite chief minister, Senmut, Hatshepsut built her great temples and monuments. The two most famous still stand today. In the area of the royal tombs now known as the Valley of the Kings, west of Thebes across the Nile River, Hatshepsut built a magnificent mortuary temple called Deir el-Bahri. It is located in a flat recess against the western cliffs and is built in the form of three terraces fronted by columns of external colonnades. She sent expeditions to the limits of Egypt's world to bring back the precious metals and materials to adorn the structure, and exotic plants and trees for the terraced gardens. This superb mortuary temple, precursor of the colonnaded structures of later Greek and Roman epochs, contained a sepulchre intended for the sarcophagi of her father and herself.

To mark the jubilee year of her rule, she commissioned Senmut to take an expedition beyond the First Cataract to carve from the granite hills two gigantic blocks of stone for a pair of obelisks. She commanded that they be the largest and finest ever built and that they be placed in the colonnaded hall of Karnak Temple. The finished monuments, both carved of single blocks of granite, stood close to one hundred feet tall and each weighed almost ¾ million pounds. It can be assumed that the raw blocks from which they were carved had at least double the weight, approximately 1½ million pounds each. One can only guess at the sizes of the wooden barges necessary to float such tremendous weights two hundred miles downstream to Thebes. As a finishing touch, twelve bushels of electrum (a mixture of gold, silver, and copper) were required to gild the obelisk surfaces.

As the queen aged, her "forgotten" co-regent Thutmosis III was building alliances with nobles, priests, and commanders who resented the "female Horus" and her neglect of the empire. Whether he regained the crown by force or by the natural death of Hatshepsut is not known; but as the nation moved toward the middle of the fifteenth century B.C., the now mature, vigorous Thutmosis III regained control over the state. His hatred of Hatshepsut had grown through years of subservience. One of his first acts was to cover with masonry, or carve out, her name and figure from all the temples and monuments she had built.

Thutmosis III was a warrior and immediately took up the course of his grandfather, foreign conquest. During Hatshepsut's reign, (1489–1469 B.C.), the occupied states were allowed to regain some of their independence and had formed new alliances against Egypt. Some of the bolder rulers ignored their annual tributes to the empire and literally threw out the Egyptian governors and their garrisoned troops. The countries of western Syria were in open rebellion against the pharaoh.

In his first summer as pharaoh, Thutmosis III pulled together his rusty army and turned it north. Men and weapons were added and gradually the frightening fighting machine was rolling again under the command of one of Egypt's greatest warriors. So strong had the Syrian and Palestinian states become through the neglect of Hatshepsut that it was to take Thutmosis seventeen campaigns over a nineteen-year period to completely defeat and subjugate them. During this period Thutmosis lost not a single battle; and each winter between campaigns he returned to Thebes to give attention to his administration and temple building and to replenish his armies' needs.

He so thoroughly defeated his enemies to the north that they would not again threaten Egypt for the next three to four generations. He beat them into submission and was looked upon by them as a warrior god, untouchable, unbeatable. His name was spoken with reverence and respect, and songs and proverbs were written about him.

But Thutmosis wasn't merely a warrior. During his fifty-four years on the throne (1490–1436 B.C.) he showed his genius in all endeavors. Each campaign brought new and greater riches to Egypt from the conquered nations, and Thutmosis used much of it in tribute to Amun. Many of the towns he captured were made the property of the god, thereby furnishing a rising, steady annual income for the temples at Thebes. It became the richest city the world had known and was to provide the funds needed by Thutmosis to build his elaborate temples throughout Egypt. He restored the early temples of Karnak and the ancient sanctuaries of Memphis and Heliopolis. At the east end of Karnak, the opposite extreme from Hatshepsut's gigantic obelisks, he built magnificent colonnaded halls and his own pair of enormous obelisks. One of these still stands in the city of Constantinople; the other has not survived. He built many great obelisks, none of which remain in Egypt, most of which were destroyed. A magnificent pair which stood at the entrance of Amun's temple at Heliopolis were separated and carried off. One sits on the bank of the Thames River in London; the other is in Central Park, New York City.

Between campaigns Thutmosis toured the entire nation, checking on his administrators, commanders, and priests, counseling all as he went and inspecting the progress of his monuments and temples. He restored temples and built new ones in more than thirty cities from the Delta south into Nubia. He had great energy and an inquiring mind. Egypt now truly was an empire which was all-powerful, totally organized, and blessed with untold wealth. Thutmosis gave Egypt strength and impetus that would carry her through several generations to come.

Thutmosis III died in 1436 B.C. and was followed by his son, Amenophis II (1436–1411 B.C.), who had served as co-regent for about a year. His was a much easier reign requiring only sporadic armed forays into the foreign states. His father did the job so thoroughly that the son was able to focus most of his attentions on godly pursuits and the daily administrative functions required of a pharaoh. Amenophis II ruled for about two and a half decades; when he died, his son Thutmosis IV became king. Thutmosis IV died young after a ruling period of about nine years, and little is known of his activities. He did sire a son, Amenophis III, who was still a young boy when the double crown of Egypt was placed on his head in the year 1397 B.C.

Amenophis III was one of the last of the great Eighteenth Dynasty emperors. His rule was to cover approximately thirty-seven years (1397–1360 B.C.), a period which marked both the zenith of Egypt's opulence and power and the first signs of the weakening of the empire. The king enjoyed the luxurious life he inherited and devoted much of his time to the pomp and ceremony which went with his position. Rather than by the exercise of arms, he held the nation together by vigorous diplomacy. Chiefs of the northern and southern countries became his friends. Daughters and sons were exchanged in marriage for high administrative purposes. An active correspondence was maintained between the king and his allies. The foreign chiefs were content to share in the wealth of Egypt and felt secure under the protective tent of its armies.

This political and social intercourse had to affect traditional Egyptian culture. From everywhere came foreign princes with their retinues, laborers, skilled artists and craftsmen, warriors, weavers, musicians, and even refugees and prisoners all flocked to Egypt for the better life. Trade flourished as never before. Ships and caravans came from all points of the empire bringing new riches, materials, and tastes to the insatiable populace. Egypt became a cosmopolitan society and began to reflect these external influences in its lifestyles. Art and architecture became more daring; clothing materials and designs changed and softened; vivid colors were brought into vogue. The classical conformity of Egyptian life was being shattered.

Amenophis III carried on vigorously the building programs of his predecessors. In the southern suburb of Thebes, a village on the west bank of the Nile called Luxor, he built the magnificent colonnaded Temple of Luxor. Included was the sanctuary to the Theban trinity, Amun, Mut, and their child, Khons. He added several structures to Karnak Temple, the greatest of which was the monumental Third Pylon, a sacred lake, and another temple to Mut, goddess of Thebes. An avenue of carved stone rams with surrounding gardens connected Luxor and Karnak Temples which are approximately one and a half miles apart. On the west bank the monarch raised a great mortuary temple fronted by a pair of obelisks and two seventy-foot-tall colossi of himself. From the Delta to southern Nubia great temples were built and all the materials and resources needed were at the disposal of the king.

Amenophis introduced statuary on a grand scale. Whether this was due to an inflated vision of his stature, or to the enthusiasm of the artists and craftsmen in their attempts to portray the power of Egypt and the king, is not known. From his rule forward the sculptured figures of the pharaohs took on enormous proportions.

Another change came in the importance of the king's chief queen. Responsible for this was Amenophis's brilliant consort, Queen Tiye. All through the king's reign Tiye is closely associated in the temples and inscriptions; and sculptures of her, although considerably smaller, usually were placed alongside his. Some towns even adopted her as their local patroness. There is no question that she had great influence over Amenophis and was re-

The entrance and part of the colonnaded court at Luxor Temple. Below, the author with Ahmed Abd El-Rady.

sponsible for the effeminate characteristics creeping into Egyptian culture. Following the king's death in 1360 B.C., she became the chief advisor to her son, the new king, Amenophis IV; and as in the years of Hatshepsut, the country continued to look inward and ignored the storm clouds forming on its horizons.

Amenophis IV (1370–1353 B.C.), better known as "Akhenaten," was perhaps the most interesting of Egypt's pharaohs. More historical attention has been given to his reign than to any other because he dared to develop new directions of thought, new ideals, and a new religion. In his book *Akhenaten, Pharaoh of Egypt,* Cyril Aldred deftly defines his importance:

> Here is a Pharaoh who ostensibly broke with the sacrosanct traditions of a millennium and a half, and showed himself as a human being in the intimate circle of his family, dandling his infant daughters, kissing his wife or taking her on his knee, or leading his mother by the hand. Here is a ruler who does not appear as the all-conquering hero of gigantic size slaughtering the foes of Egypt, or as the aloof divine king greeting one of the many deities as an equal. Here was a poet who is credited with having written hymns to his God which anticipate the Psalms of David, and who introduced a new and vital art style of his own conception in which to express his novel ideas. Above all, here is a courageous innovator who abandoned the worship of the multifarious gods of Ancient Egypt in their human and animal forms and substituted for them an austere monotheism with an abstract symbol by which to represent it.[1]

Had he been born in a different time, perhaps in the peaceful wake of Thutmosis III's conquests, Amenophis IV's revolutionary thoughts and ideas might have been implanted firmly in the succeeding generations. However, trouble was brewing in the northern nations. The Hittites, Mitannis, and Hapiru were quarreling again and fighting, and the alliances formed under Amenophis III were falling apart. The Egyptian army had grown complacent and old from years of inactivity and needed a strong ruler to revitalize it and to put it into action again. But warring and feats of bravery were anathema to the new king. He was not interested in the squabbling of his neighbors and he ignored pleas for help from the allies still loyal to him. This disinterest in the army and in Egypt's external affairs would cause severe problems for his successors.

[1]Aldred, *Akhenaten,* p. 11.

Amenophis IV's chief wife was Nefertiti, a queen whom history describes as one of its most dramatic beauties. Together they lived as a couple fervently in love, dedicated to each other and to their families, and inseparable in their aims and thoughts. The third important person was Queen Mother Tiye, as was mentioned, the second indispensable woman in the king's life. He appointed both as his chief advisors. The new direction in which he was to take the nation no doubt found sympathetic support from his two most influential counselors.

Amenophis IV was a philosopher, a deep thinker. He was disturbed by the rigid conformity of the temples, the powerful practices of the priesthood and their elaborate rituals to Amun and the lesser gods. His was an inquiring mind that found infertile grounds in the bureaucracy at Thebes. He envisioned a new spirit, a single unifying force, as the creator of man and nature. That spirit and force were thought by him to be embodied in the rays of the sun, the "Aten" radiating from Amun. All that he could see in his children, his beautiful wife and mother, the flowers and trees, the animals and birds was natural and true.

These radical thoughts brought him into direct conflict with the high priests of Thebes and with the temple heads throughout the nation. Noble families felt the threat to their local gods and to their hard-gained influence and standing. And the military command was annoyed with Akhenaten's pacifism. Had he not been from a powerful royal line, the king might have been quickly deposed. But Akhenaten had great strength of character and courage and nothing could move him from his chosen direction.

Knowing that he could not win over the powerful forces lining up against him, nor quickly change the monumental temple images of Amun and the gods at Thebes, Amenophis IV made a bold decision in the sixth year of his rule. He moved the center of the kingdom about three hundred miles north of Thebes to an area called Tel el-Amarna. In honor of his new universal god, represented by the visible solar disc and its warming rays, he named the new city "Akhetaten," which meant the "Horizon of Aten," and he changed his own name to Akhenaten, "Spirit of Aten." Simultaneously he annihilated Amun and the rest of the gods, erased all references to them on monuments and temples, removed the official imprimatur of all religious sanctuaries, and deposed the entire priesthood.

To rule for the length of time he did, approximately seventeen years, Akhenaten had to have a circle of loyal adherents who converted to his new religion. Friendly foreign princes were not particularly concerned with the change and accepted it as long as their relationships with the royal house were maintained. The king steadfastly forged ahead, trying to impose his new philosophies on Egyptian life. He succeeded in building temples to Aten in Thebes, Gem-Aton in Nubia, Heliopolis, Memphis, Hermopolis, Hermothis, and in some smaller cities.

The effects on Akhenaten's religion were limited. Like the prophets and martyrs to follow in the centuries ahead, his powerful ideas would live but their implementation would languish in the slush of hard-to-change customs and tradition. The majority of the people never quite grasped the sophistication of Akhenaten's god and the new teachings; and they never did stop worshiping the old gods, especially Amun and Osiris. The old priesthood openly opposed Akhenaten and took every opportunity to subvert his policies. Military commanders and noble families who had lost favor stood in the wings waiting for the upstart to pass. Finally the weight of his battle took its toll on his frail, sickly body. About 1353 B.C. Akhenaten died and was buried in his tomb east of his beloved city.

As he fades from sight, let us consider the assessment made by James Henry Breasted in his magnificent volume, *A History of Egypt.*

Thus disappeared the most remarkable figure in earlier oriental history. To his own nation he was afterward known as "the criminal of Akhetaten"; but for us, however much we may censure him for the loss of the empire, which he allowed to slip from his fingers; however much we may condemn the fanaticism with which he pursued his aim, even to the violation of his own father's name and monuments; there died with him such a spirit as the world had never seen before,—a brave soul, undauntedly facing the momentum of immemorial tradition, and thereby stepping out from the long line of conventional and colourless Pharaohs, that he might disseminate ideas far beyond and above the capacity of his age to understand. Among the Hebrews, seven or eight hundred years later, we look for such men; but the modern world has yet adequately to value or even acquaint itself with this man, who in an age so remote and under conditions so adverse, became the world's first idealist and the world's first *individual.*[2]

[2]Breasted, p. 392.

Breasted gives several translations of hymns and poems to Aten written by Akhenaten and Nefertiti. Sensitively written and remarkable in the devotional phrases to the single deity, they are similar to later Hebrew and Christian Psalms.

THE SPLENDOUR OF ATON [ATEN]

Thy dawning is beautiful in the horizon of heaven,
O living Aton, Beginning of life!
When thou risest in the eastern horizon of heaven,
Thou fillest every land with thy beauty;
For thou are beautiful, great, glittering, high over the earth;
Thy rays, they encompass the lands, even all thou hast made;
Thou art Re, and thou has carried them all away captive;
Thou bindest them by thy love.
Though thou art afar, thy rays are on earth;
Though thou art on high, thy footprints are the day.[3]

CREATION OF MAN

Thou art he who createst the man-child in woman,
Who makest seed in man,
Who giveth life to the son in the body of his mother,
Who soothest him that he may not weep,
A nurse (even) in the womb.
Who giveth breath to animate every one that he maketh.
When he cometh forth from the body,
... on the day of his birth,
Thou openest his mouth in speech,
Thou suppliest his necessities.[4]

REVELATION TO THE KING

Thou art in my heart,
There is no other that knoweth thee,
Save thy son Ikhnaton [Ahkenaten].
Thou has made him wise in thy designs
And in thy might.
The world is in thy hand,
Even as thou hast made them.
When thou hast risen, they live;
When thou settest, they die.
For thou art duration, beyond thy mere limbs,
By thee man liveth,

[3]Ibid., p. 371.
[4]Ibid., p. 373.

And their eyes look upon thy beauty,
Until thou settest.
All labour is laid aside,
When thou settest in the west;
When thou risest, they are made to grow
. . . for the king.
Since thou didst establish the earth,
Thou has raised them up for thy son,
Who came forth from thy limbs,
The king, living in truth,
The lord of the Two Lands Nefer-khepru-Re, Wan-Re,
The son of Re, living in truth, lord of diadems,
Ikhnaton [Akhenaten], whose life is long;
(And for) the great royal wife, his beloved,
Mistress of the Two Lands, Nefer nefru aton, Nofretete [Nefertiti],
Living and flourishing for ever and ever.[5]

The lack of attention to foreign affairs by Akhenaten led to the dissolution of the northern empire. The power of the Hittites in Syria was on the increase and they were consolidating toward Egypt. The old allies and his own governors in Syria-Palestine sent countless messages to the king informing him of the new threat and imploring him to send troops to their aid. Simultaneously the shrewd Hittite princes also sent messages repeating their loyalty to the pharaoh while they struck down, one by one, the city states to the west. But as a man dedicated to peace and to the internal revolution he had wrought, Akhenaten ignored the pleas for help from his allies and chose to place his faith in the world of his enemies. Gradually the provinces in Syria and Palestine were lost to Egyptian control. The empire in western Asia again had come to an end.

The royal succession following Akhenaten's death is somewhat clouded. It is thought he appointed Semenkhkare, a younger brother, as co-regent. Semenkhkare apparently died two or three years after his older brother. Akhenaten and Nefertiti had no sons but at least six daughters are known. On the sudden departure of Semenkhkare, another even younger brother of Akhenaten took the crown, a mere nine-year-old boy named Tutankhaten ("living image of Aten"); and his marriage immediately was arranged with Ankhesenpaten ("she lives by the Aten"), second daughter of Akhenaten and Nefertiti. This was in the year 1352 B.C. The

<hr>

[5]Ibid., p. 375.

three brothers, it will be recalled, all were born of Amenophis III and Queen Tiye; Nefertiti was the daughter of the high priest Ay, chief vizier of the state.

Ay was a powerful figure. He started as a military commander and was a favorite of Amenophis III. Akhenaten and Semenkhkare relied on his counsel and added his loftier titles. He and Nefertiti became Tutankhaten's most influential advisors, and Ay ran the affairs of state as the boy-king was growing. For about three years the royal family steadfastly supported Aten and remained at Tel el-Amarna; but divisions within the ruling classes widened and pressure continued to build for the reinstatement of the old gods and Amun. Finally the family conceded and the throne was moved back to Thebes. On the advice of his advisors the king changed his name to Tutankhamun, his queen's to Ankhesenamun. Akhetaten was abandoned.

For a short period Tutankhamun retained some of his loyalty to Aten and even restored and enlarged the Aten Temple at Karnak; but soon he was forced by the priests to rededicate himself to Amun and to the worship rituals of Amun. Now understanding the wisdom and expediency of cooperation, Tutankhamun apostacized and began a campaign of expunging Akhenaten's temples and works while simultaneously restoring temples of Amun throughout the country.

Nefertiti died soon after Tutankhamun ascended the throne and Ay was getting old. Rising to a position of power in the nation was a military commander named Horemheb. During Akhenaten's last years, the able Horemheb had led a few meager military expeditions, but always under the handicap of the king's constraints or the lack of his support. Now in the service of Tutankhamun, Horemheb was elevated to commander in chief of the army and forged at least two military forays into Asia and Nubia. Not much land in the north was reclaimed, but for the time being the advances of the Hittites were discouraged. The south posed no serious problems. The Nubians had long been Egyptianized and the periodic small convulsions were the result of over-ambitious petty princes.

Like his older brother Akhenaten, who lived to about thirty-three, and the second in line, Semenkhkare, Tutankhamun's life and reign were short, terminated about 1343 B.C. Tutankhamun was eighteen and had ruled only about nine years. His tomb, for which preparations had begun in the western part of the Valley of the Kings, was not ready, which indicates that his death was sudden; so he was buried in the main part of the valley in a small tomb which probably had been prepared for the eventual demise of Ay. There are several theories about the boy-king's death, prompted by evidence on the mummy that he might have been murdered. But pathologists point to the similarly frail, weak bodies of the brothers, their effeminate characteristics, platycephalic skulls and other distended bodily features. Perhaps these were all abnormalities caused by incessant intermarriages, resulting in the premature deaths of the men.

Tutankhamun was not an important pharaoh in terms of his historical contributions to Egypt. That he might have remained one of the more ephemeral kings is indicated by the fact that Breasted's volume of over six hundred pages, written before the discovery of Tutankhamun's tomb, devotes less than three pages to his entire reign. His monuments and inscriptions were totally destroyed by the regimes which followed his, and he is known by no great works. The discovery of his tomb brought him posthumous fame because it is the only one which had remained virtually intact in the royal burial grounds; and it was jammed with the treasures, accouterments and personal possessions of a pharaoh from the golden age of Egypt. Had the sepulchres of the great pharaohs of Thebes been found in a similar condition, the modest tomb and treasures of the boy-king might have paled by comparison.

Tutankhamun and Ankhesenamun produced no heirs to the crown, so his reign marked the end of the long line of Thutmoside pharaohs. At the presumed urging of Horemheb, Ay, now a very old man, seized the throne by marrying Ankhesenamun, his granddaughter. Ay ruled for a short period before he died in 1339 B.C., leaving the way clear for Horemheb. The former general had tremendous internal problems to grapple with, so he was not able to mount any effective new military campaigns. Although he once had sworn fealty to Aten, he now embraced Amun and rebuilt his friendships with the powerful priests. A good part of his thirty-five years as king were spent restoring the great temples of Amun throughout Egypt while simultaneously eradicating the memory of the prior four Atenist pharaohs. The city of Akhetaten, which had been abandoned, was now completely razed and every inscribed block of stone was smashed. Aten Temple at Karnak was dismantled and its stones used as fill for three pylons Horemheb

Above: Helen Boehm studies the middle coffin of Tutankhamun at the Cairo Museum.
Below: The festive wedding of Nahed Ghorbal and Dr. Hussam Helmy in Cairo.

Colossal figures of the pharaoh were carved in sandstone at the temples of Abu Simbel, *left and below,* built by Rameses II.

Opposite page:
The main entrance to the Temple of Luxor, with its towering obelisk and great stone pharaohs. Helen Boehm points out the figure of Nefertari, knee-high to the colossus of Rameses II at the Luxor Temple.

Exterior
of the
Cairo
Museum.

Maurice Eyeington and Helen Boehm with our guides at the tomb of Tutankhamun in the Valley of the Kings. The entrance to the tomb of Rameses VI is located directly above Tutankhamun's.

added to the temple complex. Endowments of all Amun temples were restored and the populace once again was allowed to publicly worship its former gods.

Internal administration and organization had suffered severely during the prior reigns, so Horemheb's second huge task was to root out the corruption and extortion which had become a way of life among the bureaucrats. Before taking corrective actions the king first familiarized himself with the nature and extent of the evils. Then he drafted a highly detailed, extensive set of new laws to deal with these matters, along with prescribed punishments for specific crimes. He was particularly hard on fiscal and administrative officials who extorted from the poor. To implement his new laws, Horemheb removed all scoundrels from high offices and replaced them with trusted priests and other men of proved moral character. It was ironic that a former career soldier was to be remembered as the most humane of all pharaohs in the history of Egypt. He exhibited a deep concern and love for all the people in his nation.

Not a young man when he became king, Horemheb chose Rameses I, son of a trusted old comrade-in-arms, as his co-regent to assist him with his heavy responsibilities. Rameses also was advanced in age, so his son, Seti I was appointed commander in chief of the army, chief vizier, high priest and vice-regent of Upper and Lower Egypt. The Ramessides mark the beginning of the Nineteenth Dynasty which was to last approximately one hundred ten years, 1304 to 1195 B.C. Horemheb died in 1304, followed just a year later by Rameses I. Seti I became pharaoh in 1303.

The reign of Seti I, which was to last only about twelve years, was one of important accomplishments. Horemheb and Rameses I had stabilized the internal affairs of the country and had brought the restoration of temples and monuments almost to completion. Seti finished the work and then embarked on his own elaborate tributes to Amun. From north to south, in all of the revered sanctuaries, he began an ambitious program of building new temples. Simultaneously he carried forward a project which his father started and which his son, Rameses II, would complete, the great colonnaded hall at Karnak between the second and third pylons. One of the seven wonders of the ancient world, this hypostyle hall covers approximately six thousand square feet. There are 134 columns of sandstone measuring about ten feet each in diameter and standing some sixty-eight feet high; and these were capped by a ceiling of gigantic stone slabs. Decorating the columns were approximately six acres of painted relief scenes, remnants of which still can be seen today. This hall typified the continuing trend toward colossal size in architecture and sculpture started by Amenophis III and carried to the ultimate by the Ramesside kings.

Seti I built magnificent temples at Heliopolis, Memphis, Abydos, Avaris, and many others which have disappeared in time. His artists and craftsmen continued the naturalistic art of the Amarna period, combining strength with delicacy in the realistic portrayals. His battle reliefs were the most prolific yet and covered the walls of all his structures. Among the most beautiful are those which are found within his tomb in the Valley of the Kings, the largest of all tombs in the royal burial grounds. Its stairways descend approximately 375 feet into the limestone hills and lead to a maze of chambers and halls. Against the reference provided by the contents of Tutankhamun's tomb, one can only begin to imagine the riches buried with Seti I.

The king was equally occupied with his military activities. He was born of a warrior family from the Delta region; and his monumental works drew so much from the royal treasury he was determined to re-institute the annual tributes formerly paid by the once-occupied northern and southern bordering nations. He first struck to the northeast and regained control of Palestine and the southeastern Mediterranean. He didn't venture into Syria, apparently realizing that the strength of the Hittites would bog him down in an endless war in Asia. Instead he made a pact with their king, then proceeded in successive campaigns to subdue the marauding Libyans to the northwest. He consolidated his strength in Nubia and Kush, down to the Fourth Cataract, and opened a new route to the gold-bearing mountains toward the Red Sea.

With new riches again pouring into Egypt, Seti I accelerated his temple building; but the king died suddenly in 1290 B.C. before completing two of his greatest structures, a mortuary temple called Kurna on the west bank of the Nile at Thebes and the enormous cliff temple at Abu Simbel just north of the Second Cataract. These were later brought to completion by his son and successor, Rameses II.

Rameses II was not the older of Seti I's sons, but he was the most ambitious. On the death of his father he arranged a successful coup and wrenched the throne from his brother. Thus was to begin a reign which would last approximately sixty-seven years, to about the ninetieth year of this remarkable pharaoh who died in 1223 B.C. Rameses II was young and brash and determined to go down in history as Egypt's greatest king. What he lacked in intelligence and taste he more than made up for in energy and toughness. His monuments and art forms are impressive primarily because of their enormity; he did not distinguish himself politically nor diplomatically; he was not particularly skilled in the daily administrative functions incumbent upon a pharaoh; and the results of his military campaigns did not stamp him as one of history's great strategists. Yet he had tenacity, the courage of a lion, longevity, legendary fertility, and great dedication to self-promotion.

Rameses II's plan of action duplicated that of his great ancestor Thutmosis III. Seti I had re-acquired only one-third of the empire Thutmosis had secured; and that became tenuous as the Hittites and Libyans rebuilt their armies. Unlike his wise father who avoided a protracted, enervating war in the northeast, Rameses plunged ahead with his armies. After about fifteen years of fighting weary campaigns, at the loss of great resources and men, it is doubtful that he reclaimed much more territory than Seti I had. The Hittite king died at this time; and his son and Rameses, realizing the futility of the annual warring, arranged a peace and a treaty of friendship. The bonds of peace were further secured by Rameses' marriage to at least one of the Hittite king's daughters. Throughout the remainder of Rameses' long reign the treaty held up and even carried over into his successor's reign.

The wars in the north had forced the early Nineteenth Dynasty kings to spend most of their time in the Delta rather than make repeated time-consuming trips several hundred miles south to Thebes. Gradually Delta cities became the real centers of power and of governmental affairs while Thebes remained the religious capital.

Rameses did not ignore the south, however; and now, in peace time, the entire kingdom was to feel his energetic spirit. Rameses' building programs dwarfed those of his father and of the kings before him, and the gods allowed him a long life and rule to see most of his projects to fruition. Unfortunately future conflicts and invasions in the north would destroy his magnificent temples and statuary in the Delta area; and only scant remains have survived in Memphis further south. The evidence of Rameses' projects, as with most of the ancient treasures of Egypt, exhibit themselves in the deep south. Preserving sand and silt of the centuries, the dry, hot climate and reduced activity helped spare many of the great works from decay and destruction.

First Rameses dutifully completed his father's important buildings, the great colonnaded hall at Karnak, the Temple of Abydos, and Seti I's mortuary temple in Kurna. Then the king proceeded to make his presence known in every important temple complex. Impatient to see his name and glories inscribed and painted on massive walls and his buildings brought to completion, Rameses II desecrated and tore down many of the ancient structures of Egypt. For his temple at Memphis he gathered materials from the building of King Teti of the Sixth Dynasty; at Heracleopolis he ransacked the pyramid of Sesostris II; in the Delta he violated the monuments of the Middle Kingdom; even at Luxor Temple he had the temerity to raze the granite chapel of one of Egypt's greatest kings, Thutmosis III, reusing the materials, with Thutmosis's name turned inward, for his additions at Luxor. No one dared oppose him.

Even without his blasphemous activities, however, Rameses II would have been remembered as Egypt's most prolific builder, as the size and number of his legitimate projects still would have surpassed the works of any of his ancestors. Colossal statues, obelisks, temples, and pylons went up everywhere. In the city of Tanis alone he erected fourteen obelisks among his temples! Nubia was gifted with six grand temples including the great rock temple at Abu Simbel, started by his father, but finished by Rameses in his own image.

There was another large influx of foreign peoples into Egypt during this Nineteenth Dynasty, providing the labor for these massive projects and keeping commerce at a level of activity high enough to produce the needed revenues. Many were slaves captured in neighboring countries, others were highly skilled artists and craftsmen. Mercenary soldiers joined the ranks of the army in increasing numbers, thereby allowing Egyptians to return to their homes and businesses; and the Hittite princes and families spent much of their time in "the land of bread and honey," by treaty the domain of their "brothers" and "sisters."

The effects of this immigration were to dilute the cohesiveness and energetic spirit of the Egyptian people and to blur their loyalties, conventions, even their religion. The country was further weakening because of the great increases in the ranks of the

The stone maze of Karnak Temples.

Below, studying the mummy of King Rameses II at the Cairo Museum.

priesthood and the heavy endowments each of the new temples required. These nonproductive functions were siphoning off most of the revenues and resources, at the expense of the commercial and military realms. Pleasure and self-adulation occupied most of the pharaoh's time and he ignored the growing strength of the Libyan and eastern Mediterranean tribes. In his vanity Rameses conducted an endless series of ceremonies and ostentatious royal displays throughout the nation. His harem was huge, probably numbering around one hundred fifty; and he had many wives, including, it is believed, eight of his own daughters. His claim as history's greatest progenitor hasn't seriously been challenged. He had approximately two hundred children and his Ramesside families filled the noble ranks of Egypt for the next four centuries.

No pharaoh left his stamp of Egypt more forcefully than Rameses II. For one hundred fifty years peoples of the north world refer to Egypt as "the land of Rameses." Ten later kings would rule the country under the same name, only one of whom would have some of the verve and courage of their famed ancestor. Yet the long rule of the great king was to work against Egypt's fortunes. In his waning years he had lost his vitality and should have turned the throne over to a son, or at least have named one as co-regent. Twelve of his sons died before him, and the thirteenth, Merneptah, was already advanced in years when his father died.

The sea peoples and the Libyans were pressing downward into the Delta. The Hittites were under similar pressure from the north and east and had quite enough to see to their own security. At a time when she should have been clenching her fists and devoting resources to her armies, Egypt had turned inward to her temples, to pomp and to self-gratification.

THE DECLINE

The rest of ancient Egypt's history is one of attempts at self-preservation, decadence, and finally, the fall of the empire. The expansive spirit of the nation gradually ebbed as it struggled with a succession of weak kings and the consequent waning power of the throne, a poor treasury as a result of ever-increasing temples and priests, factionalism, dependence on foreign mercenaries, and the building pressure from without. From this point onward in her history, Egypt would be on the defensive. Periodically there would be other rules of stability and prosperity under outstanding pharaohs like Rameses III (1192–1160 B.C.) of the Twentieth Dynasty, Sheshonk I (945–920 B.C.) first of a line of Libyan kings of the Twenty-second Dynasty, and Psamtik I (663–609 B.C.) of the Twenty-sixth Dynasty. The center of power would shift back and forth from north to south, from south to north, and separatist movements often would divide the nation into independently ruled regions.

Following the Ramessides, Egypt would be ruled by a succession of kings from Libya, Nubia, Assyria, Persia, Macedonia, and finally, Greece and Rome. The last native pharaohs would disappear at the end of the Thirtieth Dynasty in 341 B.C.

Thus the curtains close on the most remarkable ancient civilization known to man, a nation which thrived and held together for approximately twenty-seven hundred years, longer than recorded Christian time. Its culture dominated the eastern basin of the Mediterranean at a time when Europe was still mired in its primitive stages. The currents from east to west started here and provided roots for the cultures and civilizations to follow. In all aspects of living, the ancient Egyptians made enormous contributions. Our awareness of the historical and cultural impact of their nation can only increase as the sands along the Nile continue to reveal the splendor and plenitude of its people.

In the bazaar district of Cairo.

The Journey To Cairo

Our trip to Cairo is comfortable and efficient. We depart New York's John F. Kennedy Airport on TWA Flight 800 at 7:30 the evening of Friday, May 27. Our Boeing 747 stops in Paris where all passengers and luggage change to a 707 for the final leg to Cairo. Total flying time is about ten and a half hours and we arrive at Cairo airport at 1:30 the afternoon of the 28th.

On board with us are two large crates containing porcelain bird and animal sculptures, our gift to President and Mme. Anwar El-Sadat for Abdine Palace, official residence of Egypt's First Family. We have some concern about the successful transfer of the porcelains during our change of planes in Paris and their proper handling at Cairo airport. We are relieved when we see the crates carefully unloaded shortly after our arrival. Our new friends at the Egyptian Embassy in Washington had made thorough advance plans. We and our cargo had been expected.

On stepping from the plane we are greeted cordially by Mr. Fathy Sayed, a representative from the Ministry of Culture. Fathy, as he insists we call him, explains that he will be at our service during our stay in Cairo and will tend to our itinerary and travel. With him are two aides with cars and a small army truck. After assuring that the crates are cleared and loaded on the truck, Fathy helps us through customs to the waiting cars. I experience the only difficulty in passing customs because I am hand-carrying a box which contains Boehm books and a few small porcelain pieces to be used as spontaneous gifts for our hosts. After a short discussion, to which the leverage of his Ministry position is applied, Fathy convinces the agents that my package and I are all right.

Cairo Airport is large and teeming with activity. Tour groups from many nations are sitting about waiting for their flights to the wondrous cities to the south. Cairo had experienced a few sandstorms just before our arrival and the schedules are in some turmoil. We would experience a similar delay later on in our visit. The fine dustlike sand from the great Sahara is everywhere. Fathy explains that not even the tightest doors and windows are perfect barriers to the windblown sands. He tells us a story of a friend who drove south from Alexandria to Cairo during a violent sandstorm. By the time the friend arrived at his destination, the windward side of his car was glistening metal, the abrasive sand having totally removed the car's paint.

The drive to downtown Cairo is about twenty miles. Leaving the airport we first drive through a new section of Heliopolis lined by neat, new housing built by the government. The wide, straight roadway is divided by a medial strip with lush green vegetation. New light standards bow gracefully over the road, each one bearing a small sign advertising Rothmann or L & M cigarettes. After a few miles the new road and housing give way to the older, traditional habitations of the city. Brick and adobe houses begin to blur in their frequency and the bulbous mosques pierce the sky with their slender, graceful minarets.

Our driver Mommandu is a dark-eyed, brooding individual who seems to be cut from steel. It is soon apparent that he claims the right of way over the streets of Cairo. With abandon he careens through the crowded byways, intimidating some with his powerful Mercedes, others with his booming voice and threats. His is the way of progress, however. Somehow he manages to squeeze quickly through the horse-and-mule-drawn carts, bicycles, pedestrians, goat herds and myriad motor vehicles. We are told that there are eight million people in Cairo, a city which should comfortably accommodate two million; and most of the population is crowded into the poor, older sections.

The Hilton Hotel on the west bank of the Nile is one of the few western hostels in Cairo, and it has seen some years. It is clean and comfortable, however, and the air conditioning works. We are eager for our baths and grateful for the respite from the sun. We arrive in Cairo during a hot spell unusual for late May. The temperature is 107°F and will rise from there during our twelve-day visit. But the heat is not oppressive in the absence of humidity and evenings will turn cool.

We are on the upper floors of the hotel and the view from our balconies is beautiful. Directly below is the Nile River which, at this point, appears to be about a quarter of a mile wide. The distinctive sounds of the city filter up to us, a pleasing blend of cars, bells, boat horns, chanting workers sailing home, music from the hotel club, and recorded prayers from the nearby mosques.

Ambassador and Mrs. Ghorbal have left a note for Mrs. Boehm to call on arrival. They are having a few friends to their apartment for drinks and hors d'oeuvres, one of the several intimate gatherings prior to their daughter's wedding a few days hence. It is an opportunity for us to meet the family. About forty people are present, a good percentage of them Americans. Campari, soda, juice, and wines are served with a delectable selection of stuffed grape leaves, cheeses, wieners, soybean balls, and pastries. Prior to our departure Ambassador Ghorbal gives Mrs. Boehm a certificate stating that we are the official guests of the Egyptian government; it will be our pass to remarkable experiences as we travel through the country.

On our return to the Hilton we decide to have a light dinner before retiring. The hotel has a deluxe dining room, a casual snack shop and an Italian restaurant which features a variety of pizzas. We opt for the snack shop and have our choice of a Howard-Johnson-type menu. The cheeseburgers and french fries are good. Particularly tasty are a rich guava juice and the watermelon, grown in the Middle East.

Sunday morning, the 29th, Fathy takes us to the offices of the Organization of Egyptian Antiquities to meet its president, Dr. Mohammed Gamal El-Din Mokhtar. Dr. Mokhtar is an aesthetic man with an aura of gentility. His English is impeccable and he enjoys talking about a variety of subjects, including our prior trip through the porcelain-making areas of China. Dr. Mokhtar, a well-known Egyptologist, has traveled throughout the world in behalf of his country and its art treasures. He later will demonstrate his outstanding administrative abilities as well. Those who work in the Organization will be unanimous in their praise and respect for the excellent service Dr. Mokhtar has rendered his area of responsibility and his country.

During our one-hour meeting Mrs. Boehm shows the Doctor a sculpture we've carried to Egypt for presentation to President Sadat, our first re-creation in porcelain of one of the Tutankhamun antiquities, the "Bird in Nest." The original featured a primitively-carved wooden bird, sitting on four alabaster eggs, in a bowl-shaped alabaster nest. It is further described in the Introduction. Dr. Mokhtar is delighted with the quality and precision of the sculpture and expresses great enthusiasm for our art project. He sets forth our complete itinerary, as shown below, for the remainder of our visit in Egypt and provides a special pass which will give us free access to all museums and antiquities and the privilege of taking as many photographs as we need. There is a general ban on photography within the museums of Egypt.

MINISTRY OF CULTURE AND INFORMATION

EGYPTIAN ORGANISATION
OF ANTIQUITIES

BOARD OF DIRECTION
OFFICE OF THE PRESIDENT

وزارة الثقافة والإعلام

هيئة الآثار المصرية

مكتب رئيس مجلس الإدارة

PROGRAMME

of Mme Helen BOEHM and her Companions (May 28 - June 6)

1. -	Saturday 28th May	:	Arrival
2. -	Sunday 29th May	:	Cairo Museum Islamic Museum
3. -	Monday 30th May	: (	Meeting His Excellency the Minister
4. -	Tuesday 31th May	: (	Alexandria
5. -	Wednesday 1st June	: (	Visiting Sites and Monuments
6. -	Thursday 2nd June	:	Meeting His Excellency the President
7. -	Friday 3rd June	:	Abou-Simbel Aswan
8. -	Saturday 4th June	:	Luxor
9. -	Sunday 5th June	:	Luxor - Cairo
10. -	Monday 6th June	:	Leaving

We are anxious to begin our studies in the Cairo Museum, but first we must go to Abdine Palace to meet Mme. Sadat and to unpack and place the sculptures we brought as gifts. The Palace is a magnificent building right in the center of the new section of the city. It is not big and ostentatious but modest in size and beautifully appointed and maintained. Lush gardens surround the Palace on a plot of approximately one acre. Security arrangements are thorough, about the same as one would experience when visiting our White House. The Sadats perform all their official functions here at Abdine; they also have a home in Gizeh about ten miles out of the city.

Mme. Sadat is strikingly beautiful and warmly gracious in her greeting. Her stature is regal and her fair complexion accentuates dark pharaonic eyes. She combines the attractive qualities of her English-born mother and Egyptian father. Her meeting with Helen Boehm is electrical. Each feels the strong presence of the other. Their conversation is open and expressive, two women of the world obviously relishing each other's thoughts and ideas and all too aware of the fact that their busy lives would allow them only moments together.

Before we begin uncrating the porcelains, Mme. Sadat invites us to sit and talk in the exquisite French-appointed drawing room. Guava, orange juice, and lemonade are served and the First Lady proudly introduces us to her one-year-old grandson and a newborn puppy, a one-week-old griffon. She obviously enjoys her role in the family structure and tells us all about her children and husband. This leads to a discussion about the proper role of women in today's world. Mme. Sadat's commitment to equal rights is well known and is quite remarkable when one considers the comparatively low status of Egyptian women as measured

At Abdine Palace Mrs. Boehm and Mme. Sadat
discuss a Boehm porcelain sculpture.

against progress of women in the West. But her interest is not provincial. This is her pet extra-national project and she is eager to talk about the subject. She regrets that some women have misconceptions about her position on equal rights and describes a few of her experiences at international conferences. She expresses her credo simply and forcefully. "Representatives of the women's liberation movement anticipate that I am one of them in the radical sense. This is unfortunate because they are extremely disappointed when they learn I am not. I am for equal rights in work and in other aspects of living, but I firmly believe that the man still must have the decisive role in the family structure. It is the traditional, healthy way."

Knowing that Mme. Sadat is in the midst of taking final Cairo University exams for higher degrees, Mrs. Boehm jokingly asks if her husband will address her as "Doctor" when Mme. Sadat is awarded her Ph.D. Laughing, she replies, "I strongly doubt that!"

Presuming that we will not have the honor of meeting President Sadat, who currently is out of the city, Mrs. Boehm suggests that we leave the "Bird in Nest" at the Palace for him. Mme. Sadat prefers, however, that Mrs. Boehm retain the gift for personal presentation to the President. She and her husband would like us to have dinner with them one evening at the Palace when we return from the southern cities. She says, "The President wants personally to greet you and to thank you for what you are doing for Egypt."

We finally set to work unpacking the delicate porcelains. House aides bring the interior boxes from the packing crates into the library and shortly we are in a sea of styrofoam pellets. Mme. Sadat is fascinated with the methods and materials of packaging fragile porcelains and anxiously awaits the emergence of each sculpture from the foam. She admires art ceramics as attested by the filled breakfronts and curio cabinets throughout the Palace. With great excitement she and Mrs. Boehm remove European porcelains and artifacts from the two focal niches in the drawing room and carefully place our porcelains. The stately Peregrine Falcon, national symbol of Egypt ("Horus" the sun-god of its ancient history), is given a position of honor in the circular foyer.

An hour and a half has passed and an anxious secretary reminds the First Lady that she must receive another group of guests waiting in an adjacent room. Prior to departing, Mrs. Boehm tells Mme. Sadat of our plans to publish a report on our trip to "The

Opposite, Mme. Sadat, Mrs. Boehm, the author, and Maurice Eyeington at Abdine Palace.

Land of Tutankhamun" and asks if she would honor us by writing a foreword for it. Without hesitation Mme. Sadat says, "I would be happy to do so, but only if you feel confident I could do it well enough for you." Within a month after our eventual return from Egypt we would receive the First Lady's foreword, sensitively and eloquently written.

Of the many remarkable people we were to meet in Egypt, Jehan Sadat stands out. She represents the new face of Egypt—sensitive, attractive, Western in her appearance and attitudes, yet cognizant and proud of her country and its people, of the hard work and determination necessary to move Egypt forward in the community of nations. She embodies hope for the future, the sense of promise that we feel among the people as we travel the Nile. Her expressions of friendship, shared and proclaimed by her husband, are to be experienced everywhere in Egypt, "Welcome" is the standard English greeting printed on banners and billboards around the country and pronounced by all the people to Western visitors.

From Abdine Palace Fathy drives us to the Cairo Museum where we are introduced to Dr. Ali Hassan, Director-General of the Museum, and Mr. Mohammed Mohssen, its Vice President. Both are Egyptologists. Dr. Hassen, formerly a professor at the University of Cairo, is jovial and extremely gracious. He is enthusiastic about our work and purpose and offers us the complete cooperation of his staff. Mr. Mohssen familiarizes us with the museum, then he lets us roam freely. The security is heavy. In the Tutankhamun section alone, which is about a quarter of an acre in area, we count six guards on duty.

The Cairo Museum is a stately building, but it is old, seventy-seven years we are told. Total display space covers about five acres. Lighting is barely adequate. Legends in both English and Arabic are readable but sporadic. The chronology of the collection spans the Pre-Dynastic to the Ptolemaic periods. Refurbishing and reorganization are needed. Some of the funds generated by the ancient Tutankhamun exhibitions in the States will go to the museum for this program.

Despite its shortcomings, the museum has great charm and is unlike any other we've seen. The austere gigantic figures stand side by side vying for display space, a maze of stone in all colors and compositions from the softest alabasters to the hardest dioritic granites. So many must have consumed the lifetimes of their creative stone cutters, chipping away with their inadequate copper and stone tools. What a tremendous expenditure of energy in just one small room of this museum—effort and creativity that are magnified enormously when placed in their proper time frames several thousand years ago. And yet what we see here will be dwarfed by the colossi we are later to experience along the banks of the Nile.

The Tutankhamun collection is housed on the second floor. On entering the large display room for the first time, we are immediately struck by the opulence of the collection, the dominance of gold, and we recall archaeologist Howard Carter's words when on November 26, 1922, he peered into the boy-king's tomb and whispered, " . . . gold, everywhere the glint of gold." These superb treasures have the same effect on us and on all of the visitors in the room. One experiences a feeling of reverence or solemnity when overwhelmed by such excellence, and all conversations are in barely audible, whispered words.

We quickly surveyed the subjects in the collection, approximately five thousand in all. Then we start at the beginning again to pause at each case, devoting the major part of our time to the antiquities that relate to our porcelain re-creations: the Golden Throne, Bird in Nest, Faience Cup, God Anubis, Cheetah Head, Horus, life-size Tomb Guards, and a pair of Falcons with Standards. With the aid of a curator we photograph the pieces, and Maurice Eyeington takes notes of dimensions and sculptural characteristics the camera may miss.

What is difficult to comprehend is that all of what we are seeing, plus the fifty–five pieces on exhibition in the United States, were contained within the tomb of the king. The four small rooms which comprise the tomb, Antechamber, Annex, Burial Chamber, and Treasury approximate an area 45 feet by 65 feet with a ceiling of about 11 feet. By itself the great gilded shrine, into which three successively smaller shrines and the sarcophagus were placed, measures 17 feet long, 11 feet wide, and 9 feet high. Try to picture these other objects in the tomb:

3 animal-sides couches of single-bed dimensions
4 chariots
the throne and several chairs
chests
8 large figures like Selket which are 2 to 3 feet tall
2 life-size figures of the king

the Canopic Chest which is 6 x 5 x 4 feet
a flotilla of model boats
40 pottery wine jars
35 large alabaster jugs for oils and unguents
116 baskets of fruit
a number of large sledges
over 4,000 other, smaller subjects

Among these smaller subjects were 413 shawabty figures. These are marvelously carved statuettes which average about a foot tall. They vary in quality and materials, but most are of wood. These were placed in the tomb to answer for the king in the afterworld and, if Osiris so commanded, to take care of all chores that might be assigned to the king. The ideal number of shawabtys is 401, one for each day of the 365-day year and 36 foremen to direct these workers. It is not known why Tutankhamun had more, although some Egyptologists believe the other twelve represent higher managers for each month of the year. Seti I, the pharaoh who ruled about forty years after Tutankhamun, had seven hundred in his tomb, probably more than most of the kings of ancient Egypt.

A major impact of the Tutankhamun collection is its severe divergence from traditional design. Prior to the influence of Akhenaten, Egyptian pharaohs looked to their craftsmen for production of approved themes and images. Craftsmen worked in teams and followed traditional shapes and postures which had repeated themselves through many centuries. Their motivation was not creativity; they were not interested in aesthetics or in self-expression; and all worked anonymously. Theirs was strictly a bureaucratic function of building temples and monuments to Amun and to the pharaohs, jointly, for the populace to gaze upon constantly. The images served to remind all that the pharaohs were gods and that, while on earth, their powers were absolute.

The godlike qualities of the pharaohs called for perfect, idealized images. They were shown with youthful strength, health, and looks. Postures and attitudes were regal, confident, and without expression. Thus the "art" of ancient Egypt to the time of the Akhenaten was stereotyped, conventionalized. Indeed, rituals, ceremonies, and most life functions conformed to strict codes developed through the many generations.

Akhenaten, of course, disregarded tradition. If, as he believed, all that he saw in nature was beautiful and true, thanks to the be-

Studying one of the Tutankhamun tomb guardians, Cairo Museum.

Tutankhamun Shawabty figures.

At the Cairo Museum, front entrance.

Central Hall, Cairo Museum

Sculpture of Horus

The special pass for museums
and temples.

In the Tutankhamun collection, from the top: God Anubis, Golden Throne, the second coffin.

neficence of the Aten, his one god, then the crafts should reflect that beauty and truth. So he commanded his artisans to portray precisely what they saw. The result was the simple and beautiful realism so wonderfully expressed in the Tutankhamun collection. It captured expression and form more clearly than any art before it. Human and animal figures are lifelike; many are shown in action; the pharaoh is pictured with his bride in sensitive poses; expressions, even feelings, are evident in the forms.

Tutankhamun was the last in his illustrious family line and this probably explains the wealth of objects found in his tomb. Some must have been family heirlooms handed down from Amenophis III and Tiye, his grandparents, as well as Akhenaten and Semenkhkare, his older brothers. Even though Tutankhamun had renounced the religion and teachings of Akhenaten when he was forced by the priesthood to return to Thebes, he obviously still cherished the symbols and memories of Tel el-Amarna; and he took them to his grave so they might accompany him in the world beyond.

It is late in the afternoon when we end our first visit to the museum. It has been an exhilarating day and we are tired. Fathy, however, suggests that we might like to go shopping for an hour or so in the bazaar district located in the older section of the city. We surmise (and later it is confirmed by a shopkeeper) that the aides and drivers have a commission arrangement whereby they receive a small percentage of sales made. This does not deter us. Such is the manner of business in most countries of the world.

We are delighted with Fathy's choice. He takes us to a typical Egyptian shop called the Egypt Bazaar. It is oriented toward the tourist but has fine quality cloths; precious and semi-precious jewelry; ivory, ebony, and alabaster carvings; and re-creations of all kinds. It is a family business of three generations and the current proprietor is a young man called Mondey S. El-Gabry. Mondey is an effervescent, gracious person with a perpetual smile, all the qualities of a great salesman. He and Helen Boehm strike an immediate friendship and our "short" visit runs to about two hours. The cajoling and bargaining go on and on during which time we order pieces of gold, jewelry, and ivory and even are fitted for a selection of hand-embroidered *"galabiyas,"* the long gowns worn by both men and women.

Mondey has a selection of fine inlaid backgammon games and Mrs. Boehm puts a challenge to him. She will buy it at the labeled

With Mondey S. El-Gabry in front of his shop in Cairo.

price if she loses; he will give it to her gratis if she wins. The game goes down to the final rolls of the dice, and Mondey loses. Having told us he is a tournament player, his admiration for his new American lady-friend rises even further.

We were told by other Americans who travel to Cairo frequently that when you establish a friendship with an Egyptian, he is a friend for life. We will find this to be true as we journey through Egypt. Without the slightest embarrassment or reservation, Mondey tells us he loves us and asks if he can call us brothers and sister. We know the pact is sealed when he embraces each of us with double cheek kisses, a gesture unabashedly done when greeting or departing from Egyptian friends.

Before we leave, Mondey insists that he entertain us one evening before our trip to southern Egypt. He explains that he is of a Bedouin family and, although he has a Western-type home on the outskirts of Cairo and dresses in business suits, he and his family maintain a tent in the desert where they spend most of their weekends and some of their evenings, especially during the hot months. He tells us that his wife will prepare a Bedouin dinner and, in our honor, he will provide entertainment featuring one of the premier belly dancers in Cairo and his dancing white Arabian Stallion, "Jimmy." Jimmy is the best-known stallion in Egypt. Among his performances were those for former Presidents Nixon and Ford and Mr. Henry Kissinger. We accept Mondey's invitation enthusiastically and will look forward to June 1st, the evening we will spend with him and his family in his Bedouin tent.

On returning to the Hilton we decide again to eat in the casual restaurant so we can retire early. Mrs. Boehm is anxious to try the specialty of the menu, *Spaghetti Bolognese.* In one of her meetings with the principals of the Metropolitan Museum of Art prior to our trip, Mr. Thomas Hoving, then director, recommended that we try this selection with an Egyptian beer called Stela. A good recommendation, this was to be our often-repeated fare while at the Hilton.

The next morning, Monday, May 30, we have our second meeting with Dr. Mokhtar at the Organization of Egyptian Antiquities. He has arranged for us to see the workshops of the organization, to meet his other colleagues and to visit another museum, given time. Present is a friend we met at the National Gallery in Washington, D.C. when we first saw the Tutankhamun collection, Dr. Ibrahim El-Nawawe, formerly First Curator of the Cairo Museum. Dr. Nawawe has since been promoted to a new position as director of a museum outside Cairo.

In the workshops we are introduced to Mr. Ahmad El-Bagouri, an artist with a variety of talents. He is primarily the photographer and printer of the organization's publications, but he also is a sculptor. El-Bagouri, as he is called by his colleagues, invites us to his home in the old part of the city to see his work. He currently is working on plaster models of ancient royal figures such as Queen Tiye, Akhenaten, and Tutankhamun. These eventually will be cast in bronze and other metals. Of special interest is the gold effigy mask of Tutankhamun which the artist is re-creating to actual size and detail in plastic. It is a meticulous task of cutting individual strips and bits, coloring them, then adhering them to the basic plastic form. Each one requires about a year's work. The Cairo Museum shop sells them for about $5200 each. Later when driving back from the artist's home, Fathy tells us about the current wages in Cairo. Laborers who can find employment earn as little as two Egyptian pounds for a sixteen-hour day (at present the Egyptian pound is equivalent to $.70). A person of El-Bagouri's position and experience earns about eighty Egyptian pounds a month ($56.00).

After lunch we are taken to the Museum of Islamic Art, another old building which predates the Cairo Museum. Islam, which

Dr. Mohammed Gamal El-Din Mokhtar, President of the Organization of Antiquities, our official host.

translates to "submission to God's will," is the Moslem religion founded by Mohammed, its chief prophet, in 640 A.D. Moslems are monotheistic and their supreme deity is Allah. An often-heard expression in Egypt and in other lands of the Moslem religion is, *"In Shah Allah,"* "if Allah wills it." An ethereal, gracious man, Mr. Abd El-Rauf Ali Yousuf, sub-director of the Museum, takes us through the collections which consist primarily of religious art forms. Unfortunately the power is off during our visit and the small windows of the old building are of little help in illuminating the displays. Of particular interest to us are the wonderfully colored earthenware tiles which strongly identify with the mosques and other Moslem buildings.

Before dinner we are invited to a meeting with Mr. Abd El-Monem El-Sawi, Minister of Culture and Information. Many consider Mr. El-Sawi to be the second most important man in Egypt. As Minister of Information he is in charge of the press, both print and broadcast news; and he is a chief counsel and confidante of President Sadat. All the schools, museums, and monuments of Egypt are in his charge as Minister of Culture. Indeed, it was he who had to finally approve our trip to Egypt as guests of the Organization of Egyptian Antiquities. Dr. Mokhtar reports directly to Mr. El-Sawi.

The visit with the Minister is interesting. We had been told by Dr. Mokhtar, who accompanied us, that we would stay only about fifteen minutes, a meeting of mutual respect and greeting. At first, although extremely pleasant, Mr. El-Sawi appears reserved and chooses to be the listener. The indomitable Helen Boehm forges ahead in her expressive way telling him of our studios and art, of our primary purpose in coming to Egypt and of our similar trip made to the People's Republic of China two years before.

Mr. El-Sawi quickly is taken by her dynamism and before long we all are engaged in spirited conversation about Egypt, its history and art, and the state of the world. The visit extends to about an hour and a half over rich coffee and lemonade. The Minister shows us the art in his large office and takes a beautiful Egyptian earthenware vase from a shelf and presents it to Mrs. Boehm. He allows us to see architectural plans for a new art center to be built a few years hence in a prime location on the west bank of the Nile. When completed it will be called "The Sadat Center For Man's Civilization." We are shown a few of the thirty-five books he has authored, all in Arabic, on a variety of Egyptian subjects. He speaks with great pride about six new cities called "Ramaden" which are to be built around Cairo, approximately thirty miles each from the center of the city. The first, "Ramaden 10," is nearing completion. These will serve to relieve Cairo of its rapidly-growing population and congestion.

Mr. El-Sawi speaks of the state of affairs between his country and Israel without the slightest hint of deprecation or invective: "Our people have been in constant turmoil and under the stress of war for nearly two generations. It is long enough; it is too long. Now we want to be left in peace to look to the needs of our country and our people for a better life. We can live in peace in the Middle East. In time perhaps we all can even become friends. You will find, as you travel our country, that all Egyptians want these same things."

We reluctantly end our visit with Minister El-Sawi. We wish we could have spoken with him at greater length. On the way back to the hotel we talk about the free exchange of thoughts we've just had and muse about the familiar lament of mankind, "If only people could sit and talk together. . . . " As we've experienced in China and in other countries we've visited, we feel fortunate that our art and its pursuits transcend political and ideological constraints.

Mondey S. El-Gabry visits us at the hotel this evening. He has brought some of the items we purchased from him. In just twenty-four hours his goldsmiths have made a magnificent scarab pendant and matching earrings for Mrs. Boehm. Set in the pinkish-toned gold typical of Egyptian jewelry, the large scarab bodies are cut from basalt. Our *galabiyas* are not yet ready, but Mondey presents us gifts of handmade white leather slippers for our gowns. Mondey joins us for dinner. He suggests we go to the Italian Restaurant to try their very good pizza!

On Tuesday, May 31, we are scheduled to visit the area of the Great Pyramids and the Sphinx in Gizeh, but our Egyptian friends suggest we wait for another day. This day "it is too hot to climb the stones." Instead we sleep late for the first time and spend the remainder of the morning in the shops in and around the hotel.

After lunch Fathy takes us to the section of Cairo which is largely inhabited by Egyptians of the Christian faith. Christianity

Examining a pharaonic stone sculpture at the Cairo Museum. Below: The plaza in front of the Museum.

first was introduced into Egypt during the fourth century A.D. at the time the Emperor Constantine declared it to be the new state religion of the Roman Empire. In the West we refer to Egyptian Christians as Copts from the Latin word *Copticus* for "Egyptian." Copt translates in Arabic to *Quft* and *Qift* and in Greek to *Gyptios* or *Aigyptios*. In the Middle East the Egyptian Christian today is called *Quibty*.

Two institutions we visit are the Coptic Museum, which was built about 1910, and an adjacent sixteenth-century cathedral which is an interesting architectural structure combining elements of Roman and Islamic designs. The director of the museum, Mr. Mounir Basta, conducts us on our tour and explains the displays. The museum is maintained well and has large windows which allow plenty of light to enter. The Christian themes in the art and antiquities are recognizable, but the forms and figures are Egyptian in character. Mr. Basta explains that the early Coptic artists painted and sculptured Greco-Roman subjects but had only written texts to work from, thus the Egyptian styling and expression.

We return to the hotel early in the afternoon. Today we begin an ambitious project that will require several hours of our time. We are determined to send back to the States approximately thirty-five hundred postcards to family, friends, and patrons of Boehm. We brought the address labels with us, but each card has to be signed by the three of us, individually. Somehow we will find the time to complete all of them before we leave Cairo.

In the evening we dine at the deluxe Hilton restaurant. Our guests are Dr. Mokhtar and Dr. and Mrs. Ali Hassan. The cuisine and wine are good and we have a wonderful, fun-filled time. Dr. Mokhtar's personality and experiences are expansive, and both of the Hassans are Egyptologists who are well traveled. We all promise to meet again in New Orleans the middle of September when the ancient Tutankhamun exhibition opens at the New Orleans Museum.

On Wednesday, June 1, we spend a couple of hours driving around Cairo to get a better sense of the city. Early in the afternoon we are drawn again to the Cairo Museum. Its treasures create an insatiable appetite; and after each visit we find ourselves talking of antiquities we must spend more time with the next time. About three o'clock we return to the hotel and work again on our postcards as we anxiously await the evening and our visit with Mondey El-Gabry and his family at his tent.

At seven o'clock Mondey arrives with his chauffeur in a new Mercedes. His tent is one mile behind the Great Pyramid, a drive of about thirty minutes from downtown Cairo. The main road is Pyramid Street, a long, wide strip that resembles the central boulevard in Las Vegas. Mondey explains that this is where the city's night life is focused. There are twenty-seven neon-lighted, flashy clubs on the street, with more in the building process.

Once through the nightclub district we come into an attractive section of private residences. Mondey points out his home and one owned by the Sadats as we near the fringes of the desert. Suddenly, looming ahead of us, are the massive silhouettes of the great pyramids piercing the moonlit sky. The clarity and brightness of Egyptian nights provide a sensual experience unique to the desert lands. When away from the artificial lights of the city, one can discern shapes and figures far into the still desert.

As we approach Mondey's tent we are not fully prepared for what we are about to see. We anticipated a modest tent perhaps 20 feet or so square. Mondey takes great delight from our expres-

At the Coptic Museum in Cairo with Dr. Mounir Basta, Director.

sions as we step from the car to see a massive tent that measures at least 100 feet long by about 60 feet wide. Adjacent are two smaller tents, one of which houses the kitchen, the other a lavatory with flush toilets. At the entrance, which faces the moon and pyramids to the east, is a stone patio approximately 40 feet square with planters of cacti on the periphery and comfortable stools and chairs in groups.

The hot desert breezes turn comfortably cool at night and we are glad we have on our *galabiyas*. Mondey's family is waiting to meet us. Amina, his wife, is a beautiful, gracious lady with a perpetual smile. She speaks no English and Mondey proudly explains that she is just twenty-four years of age. They were married when Amina was fourteen. Then four handsome children are brought forward, three of whom are girls. Amel, the oldest, is ten and has just begun studying English. She is followed by sisters Zizi and Eman. The last-born, barely at the walking stage, is the lone boy so far. His name? Sundey, of course.

The El-Gabrys are Moslems, so Mondey does not drink alcoholic beverages. He is extremely gracious in considering his guests, however, and informs us that he did obtain a variety of whiskeys for the evening and our favorite beer, Stela. We accept the beer and find that he had kept several bottles on ice all afternoon. Ice is a luxury in the desert and probably is more costly than the beer. Mondey spared nothing in his efforts to make us happy and comfortable.

Now it is Amina's turn to welcome her guests. She proudly takes us into the tent entrance. Soft yellow lamps are strung high and cast a dim, warm light which suffuses the opulence of color within. Walls and ceiling are covered with 150-year-old tapestries woven in cottons, linens, and wools. In needlework are pharaonic designs taken from the tombs and monuments; and even the tent's supporting posts are wrapped in rich fabrics. The wooden floor is covered with Oriental rugs made of camel's wool. Around the walls are long, soft divans dotted with dozens of plush pillows; and in front of the divans are narrow tables and leather hassocks ornamented with gold-colored studs. The full spectrum of colors is dominated by red, orange, yellow, and turquoise. We stand in the center of the tent for several minutes in romantic euphoria, a feeling of well-being that will intensify as the evening proceeds.

Mondey announces that our entertainment has arrived and he

asks us to be seated on one side of the tent. He has invited Hamid, his brother, and Hamid's family to join us. After introductions they sit on the opposite side. A few moments later an ensemble of fourteen musicians and two vocalists enter from the rear of the tent and begin performing. The basic instruments are tamborines, flutes, lutes, and castanets. Starting slowly, the musicians gradually increase tempo; and at the peak of the crescendo, in bursts Nadia, one of the best known belly dancers in all of Egypt.

The tent is electrified. The staccato outbursts of the musicians are punctuated by the sensuous, spinning Nadia whose head, torso, and belly seem to move independently of one another. A heady aroma of myrrh and perfume fills the air; and through the cut-out windows Bedouin workers clap and sing with energy and glassy eyes. Mondey explains that they are high on hashish. Nadia invites Maurice, and later me, to dance with her. Any initial reluctance quickly dissolves as she slowly gyrates toward us in her encompassing, seductive beauty. Besides that, we both sensed that a man should not refuse such an invitation from so important a lady. We both made heroic, but awkward, efforts to move parts of our bodies in unaccustomed ways. Our Egyptian friends appreciated our gameness. Nadia departs just as suddenly as she had appeared, and with her the ensemble and singers. Mondey announces that Jimmy is arriving to entertain us on the patio. We sit in chairs to one side and out of the desert emerges a four-piece Bedouin group playing string instruments. In prances Jimmy and his trainer, dancing in perfect rhythm with the music. The beautiful, white Arabian stallion, with his flashing tail and mane, is decorated in gold and leather regalia and is fitted with a small, ornate saddle. After his virtuoso performance, Helen Boehm, not to be outdone by her belly-dancing colleagues and enraptured by the events of the evening, asks Mondey if she can ride Jimmy out into the desert. We implore her not to do so, knowing she has not ridden a horse in many years; but she is not to be denied. Off she goes on Jimmy's back into the desert toward the pyramids with the trainer jogging alongside. Ten minutes later she is back, exhilarated by the experience. When she now tells her tale about our trip to Egypt, Jimmy is an important part of her story.

Finally it is time to enjoy the repast that Amina and Amel have prepared for us. Egyptians eat dinner quite late, ten or eleven o'clock, preferring to wait for the cool of the evening. While we were enjoying Jimmy, our hostesses and their Bedouin cook set out a delicious buffet of charcoaled shish kebab, stuffed charcoaled turkey, onion soup, salad, unleavened bread, a ricelike food called *couscous* made of granulated wheat and flour, sweet pastries and coffee.

The evening is drawing to an end. It is difficult to express to Mondey and his family our gratitude for one of the most exceptional nights of our lives. Though it reads like a tale woven from *The Arabian Nights*, the account falls short of expressing all the friendship, pleasure, and excitement we shared. We would learn later as we traveled Egypt that few Egyptians have ever experienced an evening in a desert tent as guests of a Bedouin family. The only disappointment of the night was strictly mechanical. Our camera jammed just as Nadia began to dance and we were not able to record a single moment on film. For that, and for failing to record her moonlit romp into the Sahara on Jimmy, Helen Boehm will never forgive me.

At about one in the morning, Mondey's driver returns us to the Hilton, back to reality.

This morning, June 2, we are most privileged to have an appointment with The Honorable Herman Eilts, the United States Ambassador to Egypt. Our Egyptian friends are highly complimentary about Ambassador Eilts. He has been a career officer in the Middle East for approximately thirty years, speaks and writes Arabic and knows well the leadership structure and governmental nuances of Egypt and her neighbors. Of him Ambassador Ghorbal said to us, "We are lucky to have Herman Eilts here. He is a good friend and understands the people and problems of the Middle East."

The Ambassador is interested to learn of the purposes of our trip to Egypt and our work in the Tutankhamun project. He tells us of his personal involvement in the negotiations among Egypt, the United States, and the Egyptian Antiquities Organization. Planning for the transport of an ancient collection to the United States actually began in the mid-1960s but was interrupted by the 1967 war. Our support of Israel severely strained relations between the United States and the Arab nations, and among the casualties were the plans for the U. S. exhibition of Egyptian antiquities.

Resumption of talks concerning the Egyptian exhibition began again in 1974, as was detailed in an earlier chapter. A few organizational problems arose but were resolved quickly. They had to do with the creation of revenue during the U. S. exhibitions, how monies would be raised to cover the enormous costs, and which cultural institution in Egypt would be the beneficiary of excess revenues. The first question was complicated by the fact that certain of our museums such as The National Gallery could not charge admissions to the exhibition. This was resolved when Mr. Thomas Hoving and The Metropolitan Museum of Art proposed a program of commemorative re-creations which would be sold by our museums to generate the needed funds. The question of the beneficiary of excess revenues was between the Cairo Opera House and the Cairo Museum. This was resolved in favor of the museum.

It was a pleasure speaking with a diplomat of the caliber of Ambassador Eilts. It is comforting to know that a person of his experience and talent is representing the United States and the interests of peace in the volatile Middle East. We share the prevailing opinion that our entire diplomatic corps should be comprised of such outstanding career officers.

Our afternoon again is devoted to the Cairo Museum as it is our last opportunity for photographing and sketching prior to our trip south the next morning. Late in the afternoon we return to the Hilton to prepare for the wedding reception of Miss Nahed Ghorbal and Dr. Hussam Helmy. It is to be held in the Hilton ballroom beginning at eight o'clock. Ambassador and Mrs. Ghorbal have told us it will be an elaborate reception with approximately 750 guests. Mme. Sadat will be present. The President currently is at the Suez Canal commemorating the anniversary of its re-opening, so he cannot be at the reception.

We depart our rooms early so we can obtain a good vantage point to see the bridal party enter. The lobby is jammed with reception guests. The bridal group is led by a small native orchestra. Following are four young flower girls in white gowns, eight bridal attendants in pink, eight female dancers in multi-colored gowns with candelabra on their heads bearing lighted candles, the bride and groom in white and black, and family and friends. The party crosses the center of the ballroom and the couple are led to a platform with two elegant chairs framed in a bower-like lattice of thousands of pink tea roses. Here they are seated with the bridal attendants around them to receive friends and be photographed.

The wedding of Nahed Ghorbal and Dr. Hussam Helmy, Hilton Hotel, Cairo.

Beautifully coordinated round tables of ten are set throughout the large room which has, at one end, an elevated stage. Greetings and congratulations continue for about an hour while the orchestra plays and the remarkable dancing girls perform with the lighted candelabra balanced on their heads. A sweet punch is served in lieu of alcoholic beverages. Guests have come from many different countries and include a good representation of Americans. The atmosphere is festive and strong currents of friendship and happy conversation prevail. The fact that there are no assigned seating arrangements adds to the social interaction.

At about ten o'clock the curtains on the stage part, room lights are dimmed, and the primary entertainment of the evening begins. A group of eighteen instrumentalists accompany a male and female folk-singing couple. They are followed by the feature performer of the evening, Nagwa Fuoad, who is, we are told, the most famous belly dancer in Egypt. Unlike the dark-haired, dark-eyed, earthy Nadia, whose dancing is emotional and explosive, Nagwa is tall, light-complexioned with red hair, and her dancing is more interpretative than emotive.

At about eleven o'clock the bride and groom lead all into an adjacent large room to enjoy a magnificent buffet supper. Food displays are set against the walls with two circular tables in the center. Ice sculptures are focal points for each serving area and the delectable cuisine is built around superb displays of fish, turkey and other fowl, ham and lamb. There is little waiting and all appetites seem to be satiated.

At the conclusion of the evening a large eight-foot-tall simulated layered wedding cake is wheeled onto the stage. With a long sword the bride and groom symbolically cut the cake, removing the cap of the top layer. This releases a pair of pure white pigeons, a final expression of unity and happiness for the young couple.

At Abu Simbel, in front of
the great temple built in
Rameses II's image.

ABU SIMBEL

We are up early on Friday, June 3. Our flight to Abu Simbel will depart Cairo Airport at 6:30 A.M., so we must leave the Hilton at 5:00. Our gracious hosts have arranged for us to retain our Cairo hotel rooms during our trip south, which allows us to leave the bulk of our luggage behind. The day before Fathy had given us the necessary airline tickets and Mommandu is taking us to the airport. We have one anxious moment before we board the Egypt Air 727. We believe we have been cleared properly. We have not; and there is no time to return to the main terminal. A kindly inspector waives the requirement and ushers us aboard.

Our flight plan to Abu Simbel includes a short stop at Aswan, approximately 475 miles south of Cairo. Abu Simbel is another 175 miles below Aswan, 20 miles above the northern border of Sudan. The trip is a magnificent experience which can be surpassed only by traveling the length of the great river by boat. The morning sun merges with the golden desert sands, and sky and earth become one. Slicing through the yellow miasma in an undulating, narrow crease of green is the blue Nile. Towns and villages are few and the cultivable area of the valley appears to range from a couple of hundred yards at its narrowest points to just a few miles at its widest.

We are heading for the land of Nubia, named by the ancient Egyptians from the word *nub*, meaning "gold." "Nubia" describes an ancient land with no definable boundaries. From the time of King Menes about 3100 B.C. the Egyptians spoke of "Upper Nubia" as south of the second cataract, now northern Sudan. "Lower Nubia," which now is southern Egypt, extended between the first and second cataracts. Upper Nubia also was called Kush; Lower Nubia was known as Wawat. The rulers of Egypt coveted Nubia for its gold, copper, diorite, granite, ivory, myrrh, rare woods, cattle, and animal skins; and the fierce southern Nubians were conscripted to form the majority of the armies.

Most of the pharaohs of both Memphis and Thebes built great statues and temples in Nubia to their vanity and to their gods, to commemorate their military forays and to keep the Nubians constantly aware of the great divine powers of the royal houses. Abu Simbel, a pair of rock-cut temples built by Rameses II in the 13th century B.C., are the greatest of all. The larger temple was built in his own image and honor; the smaller one was for his wife, Ne-

fertari. Both are hewn from the face of a sandstone cliff now looking out over Lake Nasser in solemn grandeur.

Four twenty-meter-high seated statues of the king form the
front of the great temple. Below the knees around Rameses' legs
are smaller figures representing some of the members of his im-
mense family. Each sculpture of Rameses bears the double crown
of Egypt. Carvings of lotus and papyrus bound together adorn the
sides of the thrones. Capping the central door of the temple is a
figure of Re-Harakhty, god of the sun. Above it is a row of sacred
baboons raising their front paws in welcome to the rising sun.
The temple door leads to successive halls decreasing in size and
terminating in a sanctuary which houses four sitting statues of the
gods of the temple: Re-Harakhty, Ptah, Amun, and Rameses himself. The back wall is approximately fifty-five meters deep into
the solid mountain. Alignment of the temple rooms, the angle of
the gently sloping floor, and location of the sanctuary were
planned with a religious purpose. Twice a year the shrine of the
gods undergoes what is called the "wonder of the sun." On February 23 and October 23 the sun is at the precise location to send
its rays through the temple rooms into the shrine to illuminate
the faces of the four gods.

The queen's temple is about two hundred feet to the north. It is
smaller than the great temple, but finer. Queen Nefertari shares
honors with Hathor, goddess of love, beauty, and music. Six ten-
meter-high statues form the front wall, four representing the king
and two the queen. Nefertari carries on her head the sun-disc with
two feathers. King Rameses is wearing the single crown in one
statue, the double crown in two others, and the headdress of the
god Osiris in the fourth. Below these large sculptures are the smaller carved figures of the royal children. The temple rooms are
somewhat similar to those of the great temple. A hall of pillars
leads to a smaller room honoring the queen and the goddesses
Hathor and Isis. This leads finally to the sanctuary which includes
wall carvings of the king and queen, Re-Harakhty, Hathor, the
goddess Mut, and two sculptures of Hathor and King Rameses.

For many centuries the temples of Nubia escaped the ravages of
war and desecration which beset so many of the great monuments
in northern Egypt. Their isolated location below the first cataract
amidst the sands of the desert made them somewhat inaccessible
to other than the tribes and Bedouins of the south. Abu Simbel, in
fact, was "rediscovered" early in the nineteenth century. The

The smaller temple at Abu Simbel, built by Rameses II for his Queen Nefertari.

creeping sands through time had covered the temples entirely and had hidden them from view. They were forgotten until the winds uncovered the faces of the large temple in 1813 when a camel caravan led by one named Abu Simbel (Father Simbel) stumbled upon them. At the time no one knew whether they were gigantic faces of sitting or standing statues. In 1817 the sands were removed and the temples and statues once again were exposed.

Thereafter, archaeologists and Egyptologists streamed to Nubia to study and to help restore the many beautiful monuments and temples south of Aswan, six of which were built by Rameses II. The world at large, however, was still unaware of the magnificent stone structures of Nubia. But worldwide attention was focused there with the announcement in 1955 by Egyptian President Gamal Abdel Nasser that a new high dam would be constructed just south of Aswan to benefit the nation. Hydroelectric power would be doubled, annual flooding would be controlled, and with the stored water below the dam Egypt would gain two million more acres of arable land, Sudan five million more. The disadvantages were the necessary movement of people and their property from below the dam, where a gigantic lake would form, and the submersion of most of the great temples and monuments of Nubia.

The potential disastrous fate of the Nubian monuments now received international attention. Prior to the start of building the High Dam early in 1960, the Egyptian government appealed to UNESCO and to all nations of the world to join in a crash program of moving the monuments to higher locations. The world responded to the historic appeal launched by UNESCO. Many nations sent teams of archaeologists, Egyptologists, engineers, and construction crews to begin the herculean task of disassembling, and later reassembling, the most important monuments south of Aswan. The work still continues today.

By 1964 the teams had successfully moved most of the temples and shrines including those at Taffeh, Dabod, Qertassi, Dakkeh, Dandur, Muharraqa, Kalabsha, Wadi es-Sebua, Beit el-Wali, Amada, Ed-Derr and Ellesiya. The two most important temple complexes, Philae and Abu Simbel, posed the greatest problems and remained to be dealt with. Philae, which will be discussed in detail later in this journal, already had suffered from the damming of the Nile just a few miles north of the proposed site of the new High Dam. Around the turn of the century the British built the old Aswan Dam, a structure over a mile long and 130 feet high which flooded the Nile 140 miles back to the Sudanese border. Philae Island, located just south of the old dam, was submerged nine months of the year during the high waters. The new High Dam, located south of Philae Island, would submerge the magnificent temple structure permanently. It would raise the trapped waters two hundred feet higher than the old dam and would form a new lake stretching three hundred miles to the south. Philae would be trapped in the reservoir formed between the two dams.

Philae and Abu Simbel could not be rescued simultaneously. The decision was made to allow Philae to be submerged and to deal with it last. The UNESCO teams and Egyptian government pooled their resources and men in a race against time and the rising waters. In January 1960 construction on the new High Dam had begun. By May 1964 the new lake began to form and the waters crept up toward the cliff temples. It was determined that the Abu Simbel temples and their supporting sandstone cliffs would have to be moved two hundred meters back and up from its original site. This represented perhaps the largest, most hazardous restoration project of all time.

First a cofferdam had to be quickly built in front of the temples to hold back the rising waters of Lake Nasser. It would have to be four hundred yards long and contain about 372,000 cubic meters of rock debris and sand. There was not sufficient time for the engineers to calculate the highest point to which the waters would climb against the dam and the exact pressure it would exert. Fortunately their projections were correct. The cofferdam was completed just in time as the waters rose to a bare two feet from the top before they peaked. This was accomplished by 1965.

The first procedure was to remove the tons of stone and earth from above and behind the temples. To protect the cliff sculptures from damage, they again were buried behind mountains of sand as they had been hidden for so many centuries. The temple rooms were buttressed from within to withstand the pounding above. More than 300,000 cubic meters of rock had to be removed. Once this was done, the sand again was taken away from the sculptures. Fissures and cracks were filled with modern epoxies for added strength. The statues had to be cut with handsaws to minimize vibrations and to keep the seams to a thinness of one-eighth inch. Each block weighed about thirty tons. The first of 1,050 blocks

أن هذه آمار بلاد النوبة
حماية لتراث إنساني قديم ،
وخدمة لمناصر الحضارة الإنسانية"
الدكتور ثروت عكاشة
نائب رئيس الوزراء وزير الثقافة
من كلمته في افتتاح اجتماع الدورة الدولية بالقاهرة
٨ أكتوبر ١٩٦٣

"الوقائع أن هذه الآثار .. لا تخص
الشعوب التي تملكها فحسب ،
فلعالم قاطبة الحق في أن
المحافظة عليها دواماً"
الدكتور فيتورينو فيرونيزي
المدير العام لليونسكو
من كلمته الدولية ٨ مارس ١٩٦٠

"بالمحافظة على تراث الماضي إنما
نعاون في الواقع على بناء المستقبل"
رينيه ماهيو
المدير العام لليونسكو
٩ نوفمبر ١٩٦٣

**"While engaged in building
the High Dam to ensure
prosperity to the people of
the U. A. R., we remain
determined to safeguard
the Nubian monuments
and sites with a view to
preserving an ancient
human legacy and serving
human culture."**
Dr. SARWAT OKASHA
Vice-Premier and Minister of Culture
From his opening address to the Meeting of
International Experts, Cairo,
8 October 1963

**"These monuments .. do not
belong solely to the coun-
tries who hold them in trust.
The whole world has the
right to see them endure".**
Dr. VITTORINO VERONESE
Former Director-General of UNESCO
From his address, 8 March 1960

**"Through this restoration
of the past we have indeed
helped to build the future
of mankind."**
RENE MAHEU
Director-General of UNESCO
From his address to the Meeting of Member
States, in Cairo, 9 November 1963

بسم الله الرحمن الرحيم
تم بحمد الله وعونه
في يوم ٢٩ جمادى الآخرة ١٣٨٨ الموافق ٢٢ سبتمبر ١٩٦٨
أن تفضل بإزاحة الستار عن هذه اللوحة التذكارية
السيد الرئيس جمال عبد الناصر
رئيس الجمهورية العربية المتحدة
احتفالاً بإنقاذ معبدي رمسيس الثاني في «أبوسمبل» وإعادة إقامتهما
في هذا المكان ، واعتزازاً بالتضامن الدولي لإنقاذ تراث الإنسان بعد
إقامة السد العالي في أسوان لتحقيق الرفاهية والرخاء لشعب مصر .
وذلك بالتعاون مع هيئة اليونسكو

In the name of God, the Compassionate, the Merciful.
On 29 Gumada al-Akhira A.H. 1388 – 22 September A.D. 1968
with God's help,

GAMAL ABDUL-NASSER
PRESIDENT OF THE UNITED ARAB REPUBLIC,

Unveiled this commemorative plaque to honour both the safeguarding
of the two temples of Ramses II at Abu Simbel with their reconstruction
on that site, and also as a memorial of international collaboration for
preserving a human heritage, after the building of the High Dam at
Aswan to ensure welfare and prosperity for the people of Egypt.

This task has been achieved through cooperation with **UNESCO** was cut early in May 1965. The temples were cut, moved, and reassembled by mid-1968. Total cost of the project was estimated at forty million dollars.

Our visit to Abu Simbel consumes just a few hours. The plane remains at the small airport while all guests load into two buses for the ten-minute ride to the site. Our small party is greeted by the assistant chief of antiquities for Abu Simbel, Mr. Abd Al Mulla. He and a colleague invite us to go with them in a station wagon.

We are in the summer season when only one morning flight comes in each day, two on Saturdays. During the cool months of November to April when tourism is heaviest, five flights come in each day. A small village has been erected adjacent to the air strip. It began to develop when the construction teams started their work in 1964. Now there is a fine hotel, hospital, club, cinema, swimming pool, power station, small harbor, and a few shops. Most are closed during the summer.

We arrive at the temples at about ten o'clock and already it is terribly hot. A few of the guests seem on the verge of collapse and are led to one of the few shade trees on the site. The cool temple rooms are a relief and we thoroughly enjoy seeing and hearing about the great Rameses, his gods and his enormous family. The visit lasts about two hours and we are returned to our plane at midday. We are told the temperature is approximately 120°F. A small airport cafe provides much-needed refreshments in the form of soft drinks and Stela beer. On board a sandwich is served which seems to have baked dry during the morning sun. The return trip to Aswan is only about thirty minutes. The high sun now is blinding in its brightness. We are glad to land in Aswan at about one o'clock.

Opposite, Abu Simbel.

One of the pylons of Philae
Temples before its dismantling.

ASWAN AND PHILAE

We are greeted by Mr. Abdin Siam, Area Director of Nubian Antiquities. Abdin is Nubian and was educated as an Egyptologist at Cairo University. He studied under Dr. Mokhtar and was a classmate of Dr. Ali Hassan. Abdin is peppy and bright and has an excellent command of English. His clipped rapid speech is typical of the southern Egyptians. During our ride from the airport Abdin reminds us that since it is Friday, the Moslem holy day of the week, most of the monuments are closed. He suggests we rest this afternoon at our hotel and offers to take us on a tour of the city in the cooler evening hours. We are relieved. The trip and particularly Abu Simbel have taken their toll on us.

We stay at the Cataract Hotel located on a rocky promontory overlooking the beautiful Nile at the First Cataract. The hotel is comprised of two buildings separated by a lovely green garden and an Olympic-sized swimming pool. One building is the original hotel built about fifty years ago. Having no air conditioning, it is not used in summer, but it would be a treat to be housed there during the cooler months. Constructed of wood and adobe colored in brown and trimmed in white, it has the appearance of a decorated chocolate cake. The new wing is ten years old with attractive rooms, modern plumbing, and good air conditioning. In its lobby are a bank office, gift shops, a hairdresser, and a large cocktail lounge. Abdin joins us for a drink before leaving. He will return at eight o'clock to escort us about town.

Three attendants in pure white *galabiyas* and turbans are assigned to each floor. They are gracious, friendly and perpetually smiling. They are always on hand to assist us in and out of our rooms and are marvelously perceptive about our poorly communicated needs. Maurice decides to rest through the afternoon. Mrs. Boehm and I head for the pool. There are only six others present, vacationers from Italy. It feels good to exercise in the surprisingly cool water. We are told not to expose ourselves to the hot sun more than fifteen minutes at a time.

At six o'clock we don fresh *galabiyas* and go to the large dining room, which can accommodate more than a hundred guests. This time of the year it is virtually empty and we are joined by only eight tourists. Nevertheless the dinner is excellent. The main course is lamb with french fries and boiled onions, accompanied by a salad, beer, and coffee. Toward the end of dinner we are offered a pure drink of grenadine, a wonderful coffee-flavored nectar. The serving is small and it is so good I ask for another glass-ful. I will learn later that the slight reluctance to give us larger servings is not due to its scarcity or cost, as the pomegranate trees from which it is derived are plentiful around the hotel. Our stewards know that its richness demands prudence in consumption at the risk of considerable digestive upset. Over the next twenty-four hours I will ruefully attest to this.

Abdin is waiting for us at the hotel entrance. He has hired a horsedrawn carriage for our night tour of the city. Aswan is large and stretches along the Nile for several miles. Its population of about 350,000 makes it by far the largest city in the south. We can see some industrial complexes on the west bank, but most people live on the eastern side. The road follows the winding river and is landscaped with grass, trees, and flowering plants. The first parallel row of shops and homes is attractive and clean. As we go east away from the river bank the roads narrow and the heavily crowded, poorer sections of the city come into view. Yet the extreme poverty of old Cairo is not seen here. Abdin confirms that the standard of living in Aswan is much higher than in other Egyptian cities, a result of the industries and jobs created by the High Dam.

Abdin and his driver meet us at 7:00 the morning of June 4. We have only part of the day in Aswan and must board a 4:00 P.M. plane to Luxor. After a rushed breakfast, we are off first to visit the remaining excavations of Philae Temple on the ancient site, then on to the new man-made island, Agilkia, where the temple complex is being reassembled. We see the old Aswan Dam built between 1898 and 1902, then turn south for about a mile to Philae Island located at the upper end of the First Cataract north of the High Dam.

The respite the day before gave us an opportunity to read more background materials on Philae Temple and its historical and religious importance; and Abdin adds vital information to our growing awareness. The island complex was begun during the Twenty-fifth Dynasty (750–656 B.C.) when a series of Ethiopian kings ruled Egypt. Pharaoh Taharqa (689–664 B.C.) built the earliest monument on the island, a granite altar dedicated to Amun. Many of the major temples of Philae (and those at Dendera, Edfu, and Esna) were built during the Ptolemaic Period (332–30 B.C.), the last dynasty of the pharaohs. With temples later added by the Greeks and Romans, Philae assumed an architectural character that was both Egyptian and Greco-Roman.

Ptolemies were Greeks from Macedonia who entered the history of Egypt when Alexander the Great drove out the dreaded Persians who had ruled Egypt from about 525 B.C. The great liberator was received kindly by the Egyptians who quickly adopted the Macedonian king as their own. Alexander was declared the son of Amun as were the fifteen Ptolemies who followed him. The last was Ptolemy XV Caesarion, son of the famous Cleopatra VII (there were six Cleopatras before her) and Julius Caesar. On his death in 30 B.C. the rule of the pharaohs ended, and Egypt and Cleopatra came under the control of Rome as it entered into Christian time.

Philae, therefore, spans a unique period in Egyptian history and combines temples and monuments that reflect a transition through about ten centuries. Primary gods evolved from Amun, Osiris, and Isis. The God Serapis, introduced from Greece by Ptolemy I, became a combination of Osiris and Zeus. Serapis also represented the trinity (Osiris-Zeus, Isis-Hathor, and Horus). Later Greek counterparts of Osiris and Isis were Dionysius and Aphrodite. The city of Alexandria, named after the great conqueror, became the center of new religious concepts. Travelers came from all over the world and the Egyptians were quick to adopt and assimilate foreign gods with their own.

The religious concepts of life after death, unselfish love, denial of self, the trinity, orders of monks and priests, rituals of the altar, and sacrificial acts for love and brotherhood all carried from ancient Egypt through the Ptolemaic Period and led to the basic tenets of Christianity. The Christian belief in God the Father, the Mother Mary and the Son Jesus gained strength and eventually caused the demise of the Egyptian-Greco-Roman gods. Christianity was declared the official state religion by Emperor Constantine in the year 331 A.D. From that time forward the gods, the civilization, even the language of ancient Egypt were deprecated and declared illegal. Copts (Egyptian Christians) tore down monuments and temples of the "pagan gods" and defaced the sculptures and carved inscriptions.

The later advent of the Moslem religion, begun by Mohammed in 640 A.D., further denied and declared sacrilegious the worship of the old animal and pharaonic gods. Religions of the ancient civilizations were dead. Egypt's early history was in jeopardy. The glories of three millennia represented in the art, architecture, and hieroglyphic writing of Egypt were ignored and scorned.

The only cult from antiquity that persisted and was tolerated through these early centuries after Christ and Mohammed was that of Isis, the mother-goddess with whom both Cleopatra and Mary, mother of Jesus, were identified; and Philae became the center for her worship. The last important temples and shrines built on the island were for Isis; and pilgrims, in decreasing numbers as time passed, continued to make the long and perilous trek south along the Nile to honor her.

This brief review of Philae's significant history points up the shock shared by archaeologists, Egyptologists, and historians when they learned the construction of the old Aswan Dam around the turn of the century would cause the island and magnificent landscape to disappear under the rising waters for three-quarters of each year. One can imagine the hue and cry when sixty years later the new High Dam threatened the "Pearl of Egypt" with complete submersion forever.

The High Dam was completed in 1971. It is approximately 2½ miles long, 370 feet high and 3300 feet thick at its base. Between 1959 and 1968 several schemes were proposed to isolate Philae from the rest of the new lake by a series of dams and barriers; but these were rejected as too costly, and the eventual solution was to move the temples stone by stone to the adjacent island of Agilkia. The new island would have to be re-shaped to the dimensions of Philae Island which is approximately 1550 feet north to south and 495 feet east to west. All the islands are of granite similar to that mined for centuries in the nearby quarries.

Operations were slow to get underway and the Philae temples were completely submerged. As with all the endangered Nubian monuments, international assistance was late in coming. To expedite cooperation, the Egyptian government and UNESCO had issued an international appeal which offered to participating countries Egyptian antiquities in return for financial support. In time, forty-four nations joined in the effort. Cost of the Philae rescue was estimated at about twelve million dollars, of which the Smithsonian Institute gave three million. Work began in March 1972 and is expected to be completed by 1979.

A cofferdam was constructed around Philae Island in the form of a double row of steel sheet piling with a twenty-foot-wide gap filled with more than 800,000 cubic yards of mud and sand. This was the most difficult task the project engineers faced. Water above the encircled island was pumped out over a period of about half a year. After drying, the temples were scrubbed and cleaned

From above: Fouad Atwa, resident engineer of the Philae project, and Abdin Siam, area director of Nubian Antiquities, discuss plans for moving the temples; Philae Temples' complex before submersion; the High Dam at Lake Nasser.

Above: The blocks of Philae Temples secured in a storage field.
Below: Re-assembly has begun on the Island of Agilkia.

and all structures were recorded by photogrammetry (photographic measuring and surveying). Then the dismantling process began. Each individual stone was laboriously separated, recorded, coded, and carried to the mainland to a secured and protected storage field.

Simultaneously the island of Agilkia was being stripped and leveled to receive the temple complex. To replicate the old island's topography, 320,000 cubic yards of granite were blasted and moved. Because the foundation stones must be laid first, and the top stones last, reassembly cannot begin until all the stones are removed from Philae.

Before stopping at Philae and Agilkia, Abdin takes us further south to see the new High Dam, one of the most impressive barriers ever built. We are told the amount of stone and cement used is the equivalent of seventeen great pyramids and that the steel required would build about the same number of Eiffel Towers. Six large intake tunnels regulate the flow of water north from the lake, emitting 15,000 cubic yards of water a second with a force that supports the largest hydroelectric stations in the world. The roar of the waters is deafening, and clouds of mist and foam obscure the base of the dam.

As we look south from the top of the dam the great lake appears to spread like a giant fan with its shores abruptly truncated by the desert sands and granite cliffs. On the north side is the reservoir between the two dams dotted by numerous small islands including Agilkia and Philae, the latter now marked by its encircling cofferdam. The mighty Nile carrying its abrasive silts at annual flood times was able to cut a path through solid crystalline granite. Everywhere we can see piles of large gray boulders, rounded and washed smooth through time, forming shapes that the imagination translates into camels, elephants, hippopotami and other creatures. Many of these loose conglomerates were assembled by slaves and workers of the early dynastic pharaohs who sought to clear the cataracts to allow their war and commercial ships to pass through. Some are perfectly shaped pyramids; others are round or square; one has a monolith rising from its center; another has one huge boulder balanced precariously at the top. Some have little green oases, others have gathered skirts of sand since the turbulent waters were stilled by man.

Abdin points in the direction of the ancient quarries from which most of the great monuments of southern Egypt were born, and which continue to give pink and brown granites, clear quartz, and micas of varying colors. The quarries helped the development of Aswan during the Old Kingdom, adding to its importance as the gateway to Nubia and central Africa. Aswan, which means "market," became the most important southern city for its strategic location, commerce, and endless supply of magnificent building materials.

From the High Dam we drive north on the east side and pause at a huge field surrounded by barbed wire fencing and "no trespassing" signs. This is the storage area for the 60,000 or so temple stone blocks, the "Cemetery of Philae," as the Egyptians call it. They stretch out for eight acres, each stone marked so it will not lose its identity and proper place in the eventual reassembly. The impression is one of a gigantic jigsaw puzzle which might have served to amuse the colossi of Rameses II and the New Kingdom pharaohs.

Just beyond the storage field on the shore opposite Philae Island we are taken into the working offices of the project engineers and their colleagues. Here in a modest temporary building the team studies the many maps, charts, and photographs of the temples and islands. Current director and resident engineer is Fouad Atwa, a highly educated and articulate professional who seems too young for the responsibility he bears. With him is Yeha Shoukry, a consulting engineer. Both are friendly and enthusiastic about their work and they are generous with their patient answers to our many questions. On hearing my Italian name and learning that Helen Boehm also is of Italian parentage, they tell us that Italian and Egyptian contractors and engineers handle most of the important rescue operations like Philae and Abu Simbel. Both peoples have centuries of experience in the skills of stonecutting, construction, and the movement of massive weights.

Behind the offices is a small, steam-driven, tuglike boat waiting to take us the hundred or so yards to Philae. Manning it are a bearded *Shellalee* (cataract Arab) in his white *galabiya* and turban, and a young boy. We circle the cofferdam twice as Abdin tells us about the work to date. Then we pause against the dam and look down into a great cavity where the temples once rested. The chugging of numerous pumps is continuous to keep the seeping waters out. Remaining on Philae are only sub-foundations that archaeologists continue to study and probe before the dam is removed and deep waters cover the ancient site for all time.

Taking the ferry across the Nile to the Theban Necropolis.

From Philae we steam about a quarter of a mile northwest to the island of Agilkia dotted by huge cranes and surrounded by barges carrying their precious cargo. Twelve hundred men are at work moving the massive weights. Construction mats and beds of sand are used to protect the stones from damage. All eyes look skyward as each block is slowly hoisted above its target, and eager hands wait to guide it gently into its new resting place. There is a sense of quiet pride as the workmen and on-site engineers go about their work, seemingly oblivious to the relentless sun, the hot stones and sands. All pause to graciously greet us, and Helen Boehm enjoys practicing her Paduanian dialect on the Italian contingent. In March 1978 the first blocks will be brought to Agilkia. By the end of the year the two largest pylons (thick trapezoid walls with inscriptions), which stand before the main Temple of Isis, will be completed.

We are sorry to have to leave Aswan and Philae. Our visit is too brief, but our mission and schedule are not flexible. Besides Abu Simbel to the south, there are many more Nubian monuments and temples to be enjoyed, seventeen of which were moved because of the encroachment of Lake Nasser; and our new friends tell us that the Nile and its environs are increasingly beautiful as one travels through the successive cataracts into the Sudan. We look forward to a future time when we may again visit these lands of haunting beauty and rare tranquillity. Most of all, we yearn to see the assembled "pearls" from Philae on their new site of Agilkia.

Interior view of the massive stone sculptures of Karnak Temples.

LUXOR AND KARNAK

We are in flight again from Aswan at about 4:00. The heat and length of the day have wearied us, but the excitement of each hour is sustaining. Now we must turn our attention to the immortal city of Thebes, our next destination. It is the climax of our trip and the place we have most looked forward to visiting from the day we became involved with the Tutankhamun experience. No city of antiquity rivals its long and magnificent reign as the greatest metropolis of mankind.

The forces of power in Egypt moved from north to south through its ancient history. Old Kingdom pharaohs (2686–2181 B.C.) were centered below the Delta near the location of contemporary Cairo. The Middle Kingdom (2040–1674 B.C.) established its seat of power 250 miles south. Thebes, located 425 miles below Cairo, gained supremacy in the New Kingdom (1567–1080 B.C.) started by the great pharaoh Amosis I. Thebes remained the capital through the subsequent periods of decadence and decline. Its conquerors treated it as the great city and assimilated its Egyptian culture and religion. In time its name was changed to the Arabic "El Uqsor," which was translated in other languages to Luxor. But even Luxor did not escape the fervor and wrath of disciples of the new religions. It suffered enormously at the hands of the Christians and Moslems. Only the blowing sands of the deserts and silts of the Nile could mercifully preserve from destruction the treasures unearthed in recent decades.

The supreme deity of Thebes was Amun-Re, the rising sun, who became the national god with the ascendency of the city built in his honor. As the pharaohs of the New Kingdom spread their power and fame through conquests and accessions of neighboring nations, Thebes became increasingly rich and entered its long period of unparalleled grandeur. Annual taxes, reparations, and tributes swelled the gigantic storehouses and treasuries. The major part of the wealth was used to house and maintain the art and architecture created to honor Amun and to finance the growing priesthood necessary to care for the temple complexes and perform the daily religious rituals. Amun's power was awesome and succeeding pharaohs, in their passion to honor him and outdo their predecessors, spent fortunes on men and materials erecting monuments. Each new construction had to be bigger, better, more lavishly adorned. Thus the insatiable appetites for granite, gold, silver, and other precious materials. At the peak of power in Thebes, Amun owned one-twelfth of the property of Egypt, 81,000 slaves, 500,000 domestic animals, 83 ships, 65 villages and, of course, all the temple complexes built in his honor.

As discussed in a prior chapter, Luxor, the "city of the living," was constructed on the east bank of the Nile, the direction equated with the rising sun, birth, and creation. Burial grounds were always to the west of the river, the Necropolis or "city of the dead." Due to the failure of the gigantic pyramids and mastabas to protect the bodies of kings from prior dynasties, the above-ground tombs were abandoned and below-ground tombs were adopted. Pharaohs of the New Kingdom selected an isolated, almost inaccessible spot a few miles from the Nile in the valley of Biban el-Moluk, popularly referred to as the "Valley of the Kings." It was here in deep, rock-cut tombs that they chose to rest in what they believed was secure isolation.

All the tombs in the Valley are similarly constructed. Steep steps first were cut deep into the limestone floor leading to a long, narrow tunnel. False entrances, passageways, and doors were added to confuse and help deter potential tomb robbers. A succession of chambers was built before the tomb room, each painted and incised with inscriptions and texts from the *Book of the Dead*. Despite the elaborate precautions and oaths of silence from those who knew the exact location of a tomb, it was not long before robbers would learn of the secret entrances. In fact, the priests, workmen, guards, and embalmers often conspired with the thieves; and all the tombs, including that of Tutankhamun, were entered not long after they were sealed.

In addition to a tomb in the Valley of the Kings, the pharaohs built mortuary temples closer to the banks of the Nile, generally where the cultivable plain ended, to focus attention away from the tombs. The Ramesseum of Rameses II, one of the great monuments in Luxor, still stands as a prime example of these funerary temples. They also served to further assure the immortality of the kings in the event their cadavers were violated. Lifelike statues were placed in the temples to receive the "Ka," the vital spirit, if the "Ba," the body spirit, was destroyed.

Temples on the east bank in Luxor and Karnak were sanctuaries for the gods, pharaohs, and priests. Placement of the temples was critical to pay proper honor to Amun and to his coterie of gods. Usually the pharaoh himself, supposedly a living god with divine powers and astral influence, would supervise the laying of the cornerstones.

Most temples have the same structural characteristics. A sacred enclosure is surrounded by brick walls. Often giant obelisks capped with electrum stand at the main entrance and behind them are two massive pylons. Through the pylons is a court which leads to a hall of large, closely spaced columns and finally to a shrine with an altar and a small statue of the god. Around the courtyard and halls were other shrines to lesser gods and rooms for storing temple equipment and religious objects. The temple ceiling consisted of closely spaced rectangular stone blocks (architraves) placed across the tops of the tall columns.

Only the pharaoh and priests were allowed into the sanctuary of Amun, the Holy of Holies, and each day religious services were performed. On special holy days the pharaoh, in essence the high priest, would conduct them. On all other days a temple priest would do it for him. The rite involved a purifying of the priest in the sacred pool, breaking a clay seal on the doors of the shrine, the use of fire and incense, prostration before the statue, prayers and hymns, offerings of food, cleansing of the statue, anointment, repurification of the room and resealing of the doors.

Luxor, the richest city of antiquities in the world, now lies just below us and, as is their practice for the enjoyment of the passengers, our pilots make a low circle around the city before beginning their landing approach. Stretching before us are the major temple complexes of Luxor and Karnak and the verdant valley, here wide and rich in its plantings. Across the river can be seen the Ramesseum, the two colossi of Amenophis III, Hatshepsut's temple at Deir el-Bahri, and the severe cliffs sheltering the Valley of the Kings. A murmur of excitement begins as all move to the plane's windows, from one side to the other, to view the magnificence below.

Our host in Luxor is another Egyptian we will come to love, Ahmed Abd El-Rady, public relations director of the Luxor Antiquities Department and a former student of Dr. Ali Hassan when both were at the University of Cairo.

We will learn that Ahmed is a person with considerable influence and popularity. Born in Luxor, he is well known in the city and relishes his role as commissioner of hospitality and good will. Flamboyant and expressive, Ahmed is an exceptional host. He will anticipate most of our desires and needs during our visit and will accommodate us with style and affection. He is waiting at the foot of the stairs as we deplane and is carrying a miniature bouquet of henna, jasmine, and roses which he presents with a flourish to Mrs. Boehm. He then leads us into the airport lounge for beer and purchases, including a scarab necklace for our lady. He appears a bit upset when we attempt to pay for the refreshments. During our visit as his guests, Ahmed will stay with us constantly and will insist that we not pay for any of our food, entertainment or accommodations.

Our first stop is the fine hotel in Luxor, the Winter Palace. This huge edifice is comprised of an old and a new wing, the former having served guests for several decades. Ahmed suggests that we check into our rooms as quickly as we can because he has a heavy itinerary for our two-day visit. In our rooms Ahmed had placed beer, bottled water, sweets, and baskets of fruit.

After freshening up, we walk out of the hotel which fronts the Nile River Road. To the right, two hundred yards away, is Luxor Temple resting in solemn grandeur and in noble contrast to the activity which passes before her. To the left of the hotel are a series of shops selling gifts and foodstuffs. Horses and carriages, flower vendors, cyclists, and taxis are numerous as the city comes to life after the midday heat. Just thirty yards from the hotel is the majestic Nile which reaches a width here of about half a mile. Native *feluccas* (sailboats) dot the waters and inactive tourist steamers lie still in dock. The bank of the river is planted with palm trees, green bushes, and flowering plants. Across the Nile the late afternoon sun drapes a golden veil over the escarpments of the western hills. Approaching the shore, a group of men returning home from work in a small boat sing incantative folk music to the muffled beat of a tympanic instrument.

Luxor is mesmerizing. Antiquities of the city permeate the atmosphere and forge a link with the present. One can sense in the people, as we did in Ahmed, a fierce pride in the glory of their past and a reluctance to accept the encroachments of modern civilization. We will learn later that the people of Luxor do not easily move away from their revered city. Most of their family names go back untold generations and they can see their roots piercing through the centuries. Dr. Mokhtar will tell us later that Ahmed is one of the stars in the Antiquities Organization and that he could assume a much more important position if he would agree to move north. But Ahmed is not interested. Luxor is his family, his spirit, his identification, his pride; and he is devoted to her.

We walk over to the Temple of Luxor, the smaller of the two great temples of Thebes. It covers about four acres. Karnak spreads over sixty acres. Luxor Temple was built largely by Amenophis III (1397–1360 B.C.), father of Akhenaten, who also built the Temple to Mut at Karnak and the mortuary temple on the west bank marked by the colossi of Memnon. Between Luxor and Karnak Temples, a stretch of a mile and a half, Amenophis built luxurious gardens and rows of stone-carved rams on both sides of the entire length of this "Avenue of the Pharaohs." The great king and his wife Tiye ruled in splendor at a time in Egypt's history when its boundaries were secure, its armies powerful, and its supremacy unchallenged. This was a trouble-free period marked by great wealth and an abundance of slave labor and precious materials. The royal couple had time to concentrate on art, architecture, horticulture, and the gods.

It was Amenophis III who traditionalized the temple design of pylons, courts, hypostyled halls, and shrines. He began to build Luxor Temple adjacent to the Nile on a site of a small temple to Amun built by pharaohs of the Twelfth Dynasty. He completed the first complex and had plans to add a second when he died. Akhenaten did not carry on his father's tributes to Amun and rebelled against the gods and Thebes, moving his center of power to Tel el-Amarna. In the process he stripped the images and names of Amun and earlier pharaohs from Luxor and Karnak temples. Tutankhamun, his youngest brother, began a restoration of the temples when he returned to Thebes and reinstated Amun as the primary god.

The major alterations to Luxor Temple were made by Rameses II. He built a large colonnaded court in front of the work of prior pharaohs and raised massive pylons, obelisks, and statues of himself at the northern end. He also altered the inscriptions to glorify himself. In the centuries that followed, the temple was subjected only to slight changes. Alexander the Great restored its walls, rebuilt the sanctuary, and worshipped Amun at Luxor. The Christians converted the chambers at the south end into a church with an altar and plastered over the inscriptions with their own tributes to Christ and their saints. Later the Moslems built a small Fatimid Mosque called Abu el Hagag which still stands in the large court.

Luxor Temple

Luxor Temple. The head is a remnant of one of the great stone figures of King Rameses II which fronted the main pylon.

Hathor (Sacred Cowhead) at Luxor Museum.

At the end of our visit to Luxor Temple it is about 7:00 and there are still three hours of daylight left, plenty of time to see more of Thebes. After a quick dinner at the hotel we drive to the Luxor Museum, a beautiful, modern structure open barely a year. It's a precursor to the proposed new Cairo Museum. Its curator is a charming, young Egyptologist, Madelaine Yassa El-Malah. Madelaine, as she insists we call her, personally escorts us through the limited, but extremely fine collections. The emphasis on Tutankhamun naturally is dominant and the total collection concentrates on the Eighteenth and Nineteenth Dynasties. The highlight for us is the original Hathor, the cow. which holds the prime exhibition location in the entrance hall. She is thirty-six inches tall, of wood decorated in gleaming black enamel and gold leaf. Her feminine, gentle countenance arrests the attention of all who enter. Maurice Eyeington takes note of subtle details our photographic references would not reveal.

It is now dark and Ahmed tells us he has one final treat for us before our day concludes. He has obtained tickets for the "Sound the Light Spectacle" at Karnak Temples. The Egyptians describe the spectacle as the joining of applied science and pure art. Sound, music, and lighting effects are harmonized to bring to life the voices, thoughts, secrets, and philosophies of the great pharaohs who built and prayed in the sanctuaries of Karnak. The first "sound and light" presentation was at the Gizeh Pyramids in 1961 and has become so popular that the Department of Antiquities is gradually installing it at other important historical sites. Karnak's presentation began in 1972. The success of these spectacles has created night tourism.

For one and a half hours we are introduced to the succession of kings and queens who ruled Egypt for two thousand years. Their gigantic stone figures are brought to life by light; and hidden voices, commensurate with their size, boom their stories of grandeur and glory. The impact on all present, three hundred or so this evening, is tremendous. Barely a whisper can be heard as we are engulfed by the historical play and experience the chilling intimidation and respectful awe demanded by these great god-kings. As we move through the seemingly endless labyrinth of pylons, courtyards, columns and shrines, our admiration of the ancient Egyptians soars, and we are humbled.

Karnak is the grand archaeological site of Egypt, a natural museum of Egyptian art which provides a blueprint especially to the power and glory of the New Kingdom pharaohs. It is a collective work which was shaped, reshaped, and improved over several centuries. The pharaohs derived from it their godlike qualities, their crowns, and their inspirations. Here they celebrated great victories, worshiped gods, stole moments of contemplation, sought comfort when troubled, revitalized their energies, and directed the construction of temples and monuments to their immortality.

Egyptologists and archaeologists have only begun to unravel the secrets of Karnak. Jealousies and rivalries often were the prime incentives in construction. Brothers strove to outdo brothers, fathers to surpass their fathers. Royal cartouches of predecessors were altered. Shrines and temples were disassembled, changed, borrowed from, defaced, destroyed, and sometimes built over or buried. Akhenaten's sun temple at Karnak provides important examples of this, and structures of the heretical king were similarly abused at Tel el-Amarna. When repairs on the ninth and tenth pylons were started, they were found to be filled with stone blocks from Akhenaten's temple. Additional blocks were found in the second pylon of Rameses II and within the foundations of the great Hypostyle Hall. About sixty thousand blocks in all have been discovered from the temple erected by Akhenaten at Karnak before he changed his capital to Tel el-Amarna.

The parade of kings through Karnak seems endless and only the works of the great pharaohs are represented. Lesser kings dared not preempt their great predecessors by altering or building among the main structures. Their weak reigns did not allow them to compete, so they built modest temples on the fringes of Karnak or at other locations along the Nile. A list of the great pharaohs at Karnak reads like a *Who's Who* of Egyptian royalty.

Entering the temple from the front (west) side, the roll call is as follows: First Pylon: Seti II's pair of obelisks; Rameses II's double row of ram-headed sphinxes; the pylon, never completed by Nubian Dynasty pharaohs; Great Court with a small temple by Rameses III; a shrine by Seti II; continuation of the row of sphinxes by Rameses II; central columns inscribed by Taharqa of the Twenty-fifth Dynasty, Psamtik II of the Twenty-sixth Dynasty and Ptolemy IV; and a monument by Sheshonk I of the Twenty-second Dynasty.

Second Pylon by Rameses II; Great Hypostyle Hall by Rameses I, Seti I, and Rameses II. This forest of columns is one of the most massive stone projects ever built. Covering about 5,000 square yards, 134 columns, each about 68 feet high, are arranged in 16 rows. The columns are ten feet in diameter at the base, terminate in bud capitals and are capped by thick architraves spaced to allow light through. It is estimated that the whole of Notre Dame Cathedral would fit within the confines of the Hypostyle Hall.

Third Pylon by Amenophis III; a pavilion and temple by Sesostris I; a shrine traced to Amenophis I, Thutmosis II and Thutmosis III; Queen Hatshepsut's temple; and in the central court, the one surviving obelisk of four built by Thutmosis I.

Fourth Pylon by Thutmosis I, followed by a colonnade by Thutmosis I. In the colonnade is one of a pair of giant obelisks by Queen Hatshepsut.

Fifth Pylon also by Thutmosis I and also followed by a colonnade built by him. Along the central passage Thutmosis III built a pair of stone chambers.

The main entrance to Luxor Temple.

Pausing for a native version of backgammon.

Above: Part of the one and a half mile long Avenue of the Pharaohs which connects Luxor and Karnak Temples.
Below: Some of the great obelisks of Karnak.

Sixth Pylon: The smallest pylon, built by Thutmosis III, leads into a building which was called the "Hall of Records." Next is a sanctuary of two chambers constructed during the early Ptolemaic Period. This is followed by a temple by Thutmosis III. Beyond the temple complex is a body of water called the "Sacred Lake."

Seventh Pylon by Thutmosis III. It begins a series of four pylons (seventh through tenth) which extend south from the central court of the main temple complex described above. The court of the seventh pylon was the site of Middle Kingdom temples. Here were excavated thousands of remnants of statues in stone, bronze, and granite. It is often referred to as the burial site of statues discarded by succeeding pharaohs.

Eighth Pylon by Queen Hatshepsut but rebuilt by Thutmosis II and Seti I. Just beyond the walls are six statues of pharaohs including Amenophis I and Thutmosis II.

Ninth and Tenth Pylons by Horemheb from blocks taken from Akhenaten's Temple to the Sun.

Beyond the Tenth Pylon is the eastern avenue of sphinxes. To its south is the temple of Mut (queen of Amun) which spans several dynasties from Amenophis III to the Ptolemies. To its west is the temple of Khons (the moon god, son of Amun and Mut) built by Rameses III and added to by succeeding pharaohs through Rameses XII. Joining the temple of Khons is the Temple of Osiris.

Throughout the temple complexes are inscriptions, reliefs, and statues of kings, queens, and gods which overlap in chronological confusion. For fifty years teams of Egyptologists have concentrated on sorting out the structures and the identifications with remarkable progress. Yet it may take another fifty years before most of the secrets and histories of Karnak are resolved.

The voices of the "sound and light" presentation say it best at the end of our one-and-a-half-hour night tour of Karnak: "We could move through these heaped ruins without reaching the heart of the mystery. Pylons, obelisks, vestibules, chambers, colonnades—dynasty after dynasty enlarged and developed the labyrinth of night. Here we must evoke the most ancient pharaohs. But the history of reigns and events seems so insignificant compared to the imperishable testimony of faith. Men are so made that they remember better the invisible than the real. Two thousand years of royal annals—festivals, mourning, battles, love stories, intrigues and expeditions—mingle here like the myriad leaves of a tree. The God Amun is the tree, and each pharaoh has merely written his name on the leaves."

THE VALLEY OF THE KINGS

This morning it is Sunday, the fifth of June. We had hoped to sleep late to recover from the preceding day, but we are scheduled to board our return flight for Cairo at 4:30 this afternoon and we still must visit the Necropolis and the Valley of the Kings. We are finished breakfast and are on the move at 8:00. Ahmed and the driver are waiting for us and suggest we take another walk through Karnak to see the temples by day and take photographs. This consumes an hour and before 10:00 we are back in front of the hotel seeking a boat to take us to the west bank of the Nile. Ahmed is irritated because the small ferry is visible across the river but stands motionless. He and other Egyptian friends holler, whistle, and wave shirts to attract the ferry pilot's attention. After about half an hour of these exercises, the pilot sees us and slowly makes the crossing. Ahmed vigorously informs him of his displeasure.

On the opposite bank another car and driver are waiting. Our first stop is one mile or so from the river where the lush green gardens abruptly end and the dry desert begins. We make a courtesy call at the office of Dr. Abo Eleyon Barakat, Chief Inspector on the west bank. The modest building is not air conditioned, but a small fan gives some relief. Dr. Barakat offers us coffee and tells us the locations under his jurisdiction which we will visit. The primary stops are Queen Hatshepsut's mortuary temple at Deir el-Bahri and the Valley of the Kings. Ahmed decides to wait for us to return to the office rather than brave the hot sun. A pleasant articulate young Egyptologist, Yehia M. Eid, is assigned to be our guide. Yehia is the Inspector of Archaeology directly under the Chief Inspector.

Across the road from the office are the colossi of Memnon, two massive stone statues that sit together in solitude facing west on the edge of a flat plain. Originally they fronted the magnificent mortuary temple of Amenophis III, but not a stone from the temple remains. The colossi are seated figures of the great king carved from sandstone and rising to a height of about forty-one feet. Although badly weathered and scarred, two smaller figures are discernible adjoining each sculpture of the king. They are believed to be his mother and his beloved Queen Tiye. The name of the statues was given by the Romans who believed they were of Memnon, legendary son of Aurora, goddess of Dawn. Each morning strange crackling sounds were heard coming from the statues, a result of the cool stones expanding in the rising temperature at dawn. The Romans thought it was Memnon greeting his goddess-mother. Continuing repairs of the cracking statues have stilled their morning greetings.

Queen Hatshepsut's great temple is only a five-minute drive further, right against the desert's western escarpment. It is an imposing, magnificent structure that stands alone in elegant splendor, united in color and harmony with the framing cliffs behind. It will be recalled that Hatshepsut was the first great queen of Egypt. She married Thutmosis II and after his death seized the throne from Thutmosis III, who after Hatshepsut's demise was to become one of Egypt's greatest warrior-kings. To secure her name in history and to prove herself equal to all the male pharaohs before her, she embarked on ambitious building programs during her twenty-year rule (1489–1469 B.C.). The mortuary temple, a terraced sanctuary with colonnaded courts, one above the other, and inclined planes leading up to the courts from center front, was designed by one of the greatest architects of ancient Egypt, Senmut, who also served as the Queen's lover, teacher, and political advisor. Shrines within the temple were dedicated to the Queen and her parents, and to Hathor and Anubis.

From the lower court in front of the temple we walk up the 15° plane to the central court which begins with two colonnades of twenty-two columns each on both sides of the entrance. Through the central court another ramp leads to the upper terrace which also is fronted by similar rows of flanking columns. The colonnade to the left was built to commemorate the successful expedition the Queen sent to the land of Punt to obtain myrrh trees and tropical plants for the terraced gardens. The other colonnade represented her right by birth to assume the throne of Egypt. Hathor's shrine is to the left of the Punt colonnade. Anubis's shrine is to the right of the birthright colonnade. Upper courts housed the altars and sanctuary rooms.

This great temple deserves the accolade, "most splendid of all"; and apart from its aesthetic appeal, Hatshepsut's Deir el-Bahri served as the model, or precursor, for much of the world's architecture that followed.

The cliffs at Deir el-Bahri are famous for another reason. In the late 1800s tomb artifacts and antiques began appearing in the Luxor markets. The flow was such that it was obvious someone had discovered a royal cache and was quietly profiting from it. Authorities worked for several years to trace the valuables to their source. Eventually a local merchant was found to be responsible, and in 1881 the investigators were led to a shaft hidden in the cliffs just to the north of Queen Hatshepsut's temple. Here were found no less than forty mummies of some of the greatest pharaohs of history including Amenophis I, Thutmosis II, Thutmosis III, Seti I, Rameses II and Rameses III. Hatshepsut's body was not among these and has never been found. It probably suffered the same fate as her inscriptions and murals, all of which were obliterated by the avenging Thutmosis III.

Tomb robbing was rampant during the New Kingdom, particularly after the radical religious changes wrought by Akhenaten. Perhaps it was one of the later Ramessides who ordered the mummies moved from the tombs to this isolated shaft in a last attempt to save the royal bodies from desecration and destruction.

We complete our visit to Deir el-Bahri at about noon. The sun now is merciless and the stones burn through the soles of our shoes. We really feel the impact of the arid remoteness, the reason why the pharaohs chose this inhospitable area for their necropolis. We are the only visitors. It is absolutely still. Not a bird, not a plant, not a living thing is in evidence. The burning, blinding sun dominates the mind and the body. Near the access road is a lean-to and a solitary guard who sits alone in a squat position. We are alarmed when we see that the car and driver are gone. The guard explains to Yehia that the driver was hot and hungry. He drove back to his village for lunch. We gather he was somewhat annoyed at having to be in the heat at a time when most reasonable Egyptians are taking a midday rest. The twenty-minute wait for his return seems like an eternity.

We are on our way to the Valley of the Kings at about 12:30. Yehia instructs the driver to pass slowly by other important monuments and burial sites which we do not have time to see thoroughly. All are within about a six mile square area. Earlier we passed Medinet Habu, a complex of mortuary temples built by Amenophis I, Hatshepsut, Thutmosis III, and Rameses III. It is located near the Valley of the Queens which lies south of Deir el-Bahri and the Valley of the Kings. Just north of Hatshepsut's temple are the great mortuary Ramesseum of Rameses II, tombs of the nobles, and the temple of Seti I. All are against, or in front of, the eastern cliffs of the Sahara. Now we are turning west up into a

Top: Queen Hatshepsut's Temple at Deir el-Bahri.
Center: The tomb entrances of King Rameses VI (upper level) and Tutankhamun.
Bottom: In front of the entrance to Tutankhamun's tomb.

winding gorge through the cliffs. The road becomes narrow and unpaved. Carpets of limestone and sandstone rubble face the steepening walls. Once through the gorge the topography flattens again to another set of hills a mile beyond. At the foot of these hills is a small valley which is oriented north to south. This is the Valley of the Kings, nestled among the highest cliffs of the Theban hills.

Our car stops at the gates to the tombs where we are delighted to see a small restaurant. Business is not brisk today. We are the only visitors. We pause for a drink of soda, then make our way into the valley. Yehia estimates the temperature here to be about 130°F. The hot stones give new life to our feet and we hurry toward the relief of the cool tombs.

Before describing the tomb of Tutankhamun and its discovery, as related by Howard Carter, it is essential to know the history of the valley. As stated, all the tombs were broken into and robbed with a few years of burial. Even Tutankhamun's was entered within ten to fifteen years after his death. By the end of the Twenty-second Dynasty, most of them had literally been stripped of their mummies and possessions and the valley and surrounding hills served other purposes through the following centuries. Their isolation and solitude alternately attracted bandits and hermits; and in the first three centuries A.D., Christians found their way to the valley for protection and peace. A complete colony of anchorites lived in the valley from the second to fourth centuries and even established their church in one of the exposed larger tombs. It is a strange and ironic twist of history that many of the hypogeums of the great pharaohs, with the riches and splendor accorded only to kings, were later used for monastics, hermits, and criminals.

The first descriptions of the valley in modern times were made by English travelers named Pococke, Norden, and Bruce who at various times visited the west bank between 1743 and 1769. They all reported finding bands of thieves and wanted criminals in the hills and valleys, and it was dangerous for them to visit the area of the tombs. Even the great Napoleon and his archaeologists at the end of the century were treated inhospitably by the tomb dwellers, and the accompanying troops could not dislodge the inhabitants from their maze of tunnels and grottos deep within the bowels of the cliffs. By the early nineteenth century local authorities finally did dislodge the colony of tomb dwellers, and thereafter no groups were allowed again to occupy the area. At this time in history, fourteen of the tombs were accessible. The others remained to be discovered under the rubble of the centuries.

One of the most remarkable excavators to work in the valley was Giovanni Battista Belzoni, an Italian giant who was known for his feats of strength. He traveled to Egypt to seek his fortune and wound up in the Valley of the Kings collecting antiquities for patrons. Between 1815 and 1820 he discovered and cleared a number of tombs including those of the pharaohs Ay, Mentukerkhepeshef, Rameses I, and Seti I. Thereafter he proclaimed there were no more tombs to be found in the valley. Of course, he was wrong.

Many other expeditions followed that of Belzoni. A German group in 1844, headed by Karl Richard Lepsius, uncovered the tomb of Rameses II. From then until the end of the century no further important discoveries were made. In 1898, Victor Loret, then Director-General of the Antiquities Service, conducted a new and thorough search on a massive scale and discovered the tombs of Thutmosis I, Rameses VI, and Amenophis II. An American, Theodore Davis, was granted the valley concession in 1902 and he and his team excavated for twelve years. They made the further significant tomb discoveries of Thutmosis IV, Hatshepsut, Soptah, Thua, Yua, Horemheb, and a vault which contained the mummy of Akhenaten which, on the destruction of his beloved Tel el-Amarna, had been transferred to the valley.

Howard Carter traveled to Egypt toward the end of the nineteenth century and, at the age of nineteen in 1891, worked at Tel el-Amarna with the great archaeologist-Egyptologist, Flinders Petrie. Carter later became Inspector of the Antiquities Department for the west bank at Thebes and actually supervised the clearing of two tombs by Davis. In the meantime, he began excavating in other places outside the valley under the patronage of Lord Carnarvon, a wealthy Englishman interested in Egyptian antiques.

In 1914 Davis gave up the concession to the valley and, like so many Egyptologists before him, stated that there were no more tombs to be found. Carter and Lord Carnarvon were not convinced of this and were granted the concession the same year as Davis relinquished it. They believed that certain areas of the valley had not been thoroughly examined, and they felt sufficient evidence existed to indicate that the tomb of the boy-king, Tutankhamun, remained to be found. The evidence consisted of several things unearthed by Davis, but ignored—a faience cup bearing Tutankhamun's cartouche, fragments of gold foil bearing the names of the king and his bride, Ankhesenamun, and clay seals of Tutankhamun found among the funerary remnants of Akhenaten.

Carter's search began in 1914, was interrupted by World War I in 1916, and resumed in 1919. The work continued through 1921 without success. Carter and his workmen had cleared every suspected area but one, a location just below the entrance to the tomb of Rameses VI, covered by debris, flint boulders, and workmen's huts. It was decided that only one more season would be devoted to the search. Five years had passed, 200,000 tons of rubble had been moved, and Lord Carnarvon had expended about half a million British pounds.

The remainder of the story became known to the world beginning on November 4, 1922, when the first step cut in the rock was unearthed. By the end of the next day, twelve steps were exposed and the upper part of the tunnel doorway appeared. In view of the potential importance of the discovery and the support given to Carter over the years by his patron, he decided to suspend further excavation until Lord Carnarvon, who was still in England, could join the team and share in the excitement. On November 23 Lord Carnarvon and his daughter arrived in Luxor. The next day the entire staircase comprised of sixteen steps was cleared, and the sealed doorway was exposed.

Careful examination of the door brought the disheartening realization that there had been two separate openings and re-sealings on its surface. Robbers had obviously passed through the door on two different occasions and the breaches were subsequently patched and re-sealed by necropolis guards. But since the door had been re-sealed and the entrance covered over with rubble, there was hope that some of the tomb contents and perhaps the sarcophagus and mummy were still intact.

By November 26 the first door had been opened and the corridor was cleared. Thirty feet from the outer door the workmen came to another door sealed exactly like the first. A small hole was made in the door, just big enough for a lighted candle to be inserted. Carter had the honor of being the first to peer in, with Lord Carnarvon anxiously waiting behind him. Here is how Carter described the experience.

At first I could see nothing, the hot air escaping from the chamber causing the candle flame to flicker, but presently, as my eyes grew accustomed to the light, details of the room within emerged slowly from the mist, strange animals, statues and gold—everywhere the glint of gold. For the moment—an eternity it must have seemed to the others standing by—I was struck dumb with amazement, and when Lord Carnarvon, unable to stand the suspense any longer, inquired anxiously, "Can you see anything?" it was all I could do to get out the words, "Yes, wonderful things."[1]

Carter goes on to describe his feelings as he looked through the hole in the door, back through thirty-three centuries of time.

I suppose most excavators would confess to a feeling of awe—embarrassment almost—when they break into a chamber closed and sealed by pious hands so many centuries ago. For the moment, time as a factor in human life has lost its meaning. Three thousand, four thousand years maybe, have passed and gone since human feet last trod the floor on which you stand, and yet, as you note the signs of recent life around you—the half-filled bowl of mortar for the door, the blackened lamp, the finger-mark upon the freshly painted surface, the farewell garland dropped upon the threshold—you feel it might have been but yesterday. The very air you breathe, unchanged throughout the centuries, you share with those who laid the mummy to its rest. Time is annihilated by little intimate details such as these, and you feel an intruder.

That is perhaps the first and dominant sensation, but others follow thick and fast—the exhilaration of discovery, the fever of suspense, the almost overmastering impulse, born of curiosity, to break down seals and lift the lids of boxes, the thought—pure joy to the investigator—that you are about to add a page to history, or solve some problem of research, the strained expectancy— why not confess it? —of the treasure-seeker. Did these thoughts actually pass through our minds at the time, or have I imagined them since? I cannot tell. It was the discovery that my memory was blank, and not the mere desire for chapter-ending, that occasioned this digression.

Surely never before in the whole history of excavation had such an amazing sight been seen as the light of our torch revealed to us. The photographs which have subsequently been published were taken afterwards when the tomb had been opened and electric light installed. Let the reader imagine how the objects appeared to us as we looked down upon them from our spy-hole in the blocked doorway, casting the beam of light from our torch—the first light that had

---

[1]Howard Carter, *Tutankhamun's Treasure*, p. 35. Copyright © 1954. Reprinted by permission of E. P. Dutton & Co. and the Julian Bach Literary Agency, Inc.

pierced the darkness of the chamber for three thousand years—from one group of objects to another, in a vain attempt to interpret the treasure that lay before us. The effect was bewildering, over-whelming. I suppose we had never formulated in our minds just what we had expected or hoped to see, but certainly we had never dreamed of anything like this—a whole museumful it seemed—of objects, some familiar, but some the like of which we had never seen, piled one upon another in seemingly endless profusion.[2]

Apart from the credit due Howard Carter, Lord Carnarvon, and their team for their magnificent discovery, the world owes them a debt for their patience in clearing the tomb in a careful and scientific manner. Resisting what must have been painful impulses to immediately search and scour the archaeological treasures of the tomb chambers, the team laid out a careful plan of recording and preserving all objects before a single piece was brought to daylight. The entire project consumed almost six years before completion. Each object had to be photographed *in situ* among the other objects, notes had to be made on its placement and condition, and its measurements taken. More photographs were needed of the individual pieces both before and after undergoing restorative and preservative treatments, and finally the objects had to be properly stored after removal from the tomb.

We think about all of this as we descend the rock-cut steps into the short, declining passage. We are struck by the simplicity of the chambers. The rooms are small and not elaborate. There are no series of corridors, hidden passages, sunken stairwells and multiple rooms as in the orthodox Theban manner. Only the walls of the burial chamber are painted with funereal and religious scenes. All that remains in the tomb is the magnificent yellow quartzite sarcophagus within which the boy-king's mummy still rests. The top of the sarcophagus now has a thick cover of glass through which we can see the wrapped mummy. Over the head is a substitute of the original effigy mask.

We linger in the tomb for about forty-five minutes while Yehia gives us additional intimate details about Tutankhamun. He is patient as we take as many photographs as we wish in the dimly lit chambers. He allows us to climb over the low barrier separating the Antechamber and Tomb Room so we can have the closest possible look at the young pharaoh. The mixed feelings of awe,

[2]Ibid., p. 38.

Entrance, stairway, and inner chamber of Tutankhamun's tomb.

admiration, and sadness which we shared when staring at the effigy mask at the National Gallery several months ago return now in fullness. We experience that indefinable sense of history described by Howard Carter. Time stands still as we silently visit with Tutankhamun, the "living image of Amun."

Yehia reminds us of our pressing schedule. We have a few moments to descend the large, elaborate tomb of Seti I adjacent and that of Rameses VI just a few feet from Tutankhamun's. At 2:00 we return to our car for the return trip to the Nile. This time the ferry is waiting and we lose no time in returning to Luxor.

On arriving at the hotel to bid farewell and pick up our baggage, Ahmed informs us that we have two messages. The first is from Dr. Mokhtar. It states that on our return to Cairo this evening we will have the honor of dining with President and Mme. Sadat. We hardly begin to express our pleasure and surprise when Ahmed reads the second message subsequently received. We cannot fly to Cairo at 4:30 as scheduled! A sudden sandstorm has closed Cairo Airport to all flights. We must stay over tonight in Luxor, which unfortunately forces us to miss the anticipated evening with the President and First Lady. We are disappointed, of course, but nothing can dim the exhilarating and rewarding experience we've had in our trip to date.

Ahmed rises to the occasion. The change in plans will allow him to show us some of the night life of Luxor, and he will plan an outstanding farewell dinner in our honor. In spite of our weariness, we know we cannot disappoint Ahmed. His smiling enthusiasm and our affection for our new friend buoy our sagging bodies. We have a wonderful time and finally return to our hotel at about midnight.

Our flight this morning, June 6, departs at 10:00. Somehow Ahmed is able to secure three good seats for us even though the plane now is overbooked. Further, he has arranged for us the additional courtesy of passing around the baggage checkpoint and personally escorts us to our seats. Ahmed embraces us and presents Mrs. Boehm with another miniature bouquet, similar to the one he gave her on our arrival two days before. His moistened eyes express his feelings and ours as he deplanes.

THE RETURN TO CAIRO

We arrive at Cairo Airport at about 11:30. Fathy and his two colleagues are waiting to greet us. Returning to the Hilton, we tend to personal matters and enjoy a much-needed rest. Dr. Mokhtar comes to the hotel at 5:30 to review our trip with us and to bid us farewell. He is leaving Cairo for a few days and our departure is scheduled early the morning of June 8. We now are "old friends" and our hour-long visit with the President of the Egyptian Organization of Antiquities is filled with fun and warmth. It is difficult to properly express our thanks for the hospitality and friendship he and his outstanding colleagues have given us during our travels through Egypt. We promise to resume our friendship at future openings of the Tutankhamun exhibition in the United States. Before leaving, Dr. Mokhtar tells us that Mme. Sadat would like to see us again tomorrow, June 7, at Abdine Palace. Otherwise our time is free until our departure.

The morning of the seventh Mrs. Boehm, Maurice Eyeington and I spend another two hours at the Cairo Museum. Our appreciation for its treasures, so intense on prior visits, is further enhanced by the experiences and increased knowledge gained over the past week. We now are confident that the objects selected for our re-creations in porcelain are the best possible choices.

Following lunch we are taken to Abdine Palace where we share with Mme. Sadat a dessert of ice cream and fruit. She is pleased that we are so fulfilled by our visit and enjoys the descriptions of our day-to-day activities in southern Egypt. We now better comprehend the current exhibition of Tutankhamun antiquities in the United States and its importance to Egypt, to international friendship, and to art appreciation. In one of her statements, Mme. Sadat perceptively assesses the contributions of Egyptian antiquities: "Without the need for written and spoken words, the antiquities serve as our strongest ambassadors for good will and understanding. No person or group of diplomats can have the impact of the Tutankhamun collection experience now going on in America. Yet we're not doing enough in sharing our art. Only in recent years have we begun to stage traveling exhibitions. We have so much more we can do."

Mme. Sadat confirms that she will write the foreword to our book about our trip. "In fact," she says, "I've already started to think about it." After allowing us to take photographs and calling in the official resident photographer to do the same, we express our gratitude and farewell to Egypt's marvelous First Lady.

On returning to the hotel we receive a call from Ambassador and Mrs. Ghorbal. They are coming to the Hilton to share with us and others the photographs taken of the wedding of their daughter and new son-in-law. It is the perfect climax to our trip. Our last few hours in Cairo are spent with the two dear friends responsible for the Boehm Journey to Egypt, Land of Tutankhamun.

Mrs. Boehm, Mme. Sadat and Mrs. Ghorbal at the wedding.

Above: Looking south from the Cataract Hotel in Aswan.
Below: Omar Khayam Hotel, part of the new Marriott Hotel presently under construction in Cairo.

Reflections

For those interested in the current state of affairs in Egypt, and those who are considering a visit there in the near future, it is useful to reflect on our observations and experiences in concluding this journal.

Egypt is a country with great potential and promise. One of the reasons why her ancient civilizations flourished and rose to unprecedented accomplishments was due to centuries of peaceful development without serious external threats to her security. This is what Egypt needs now, a few decades of peace in which to resolve her internal problems, a long enough pause to concentrate again on the unique natural gifts of its people, of the land, and of the River Nile.

The reopened Suez Canal is now bringing Egypt revenue of half a billion dollars a year. New oil reserves are being found and current consumption is less than production, allowing Egypt to begin to offset its horrendous trade deficits. A vast sea of underground water has been discovered in the western Sahara which can bring thousands of desert acres to life, providing the opportunity to build new communities that will relieve the congestion of Cairo and other Nile cities. Reserves of minerals such as iron ore and phosphates are waiting to be tapped.

Egypt is the acknowledged leader of the Arab world. Its people are energetic, proud, and peace-loving. They are leaders, educators, eclectic in their attitudes and very much aware of their importance to the world community of nations. In addition to all of this, given an assurance of peace in the Middle East, tourists will flock to Egypt to see its wonders along the Nile. There is little question that Egypt will be a major tourist mecca of the world when peace comes.

And come it will. All through Egypt we sensed a genuine desire of the people for peace, from Mme. Sadat, Minister El-Sawi, Ambassador and Mrs. Ghorbal, to the friendly guides and working people we met in our travels. President Sadat's attitudes and initiatives for peace have been fervently supported by the people, and we experienced no invective against any people or country. To the contrary, we were welcomed everywhere and we heard Egyptian after Egyptian refer to all peoples of the world as brothers and sisters.

Egypt, like other developing countries, cannot offer the deluxe accommodations of the West to the traveler today. Hotel space in Cairo and other cities is at a premium, although several new hoteliers, including the Marriott Corporation, are building huge new facilities along the Nile. Automobiles operate with difficulty because of monumental traffic jams caused by narrow streets, the mix of push carts and the crush of pedestrians. Trains and planes are adequate but operate on thin schedules. Electric, water, and telephone services fail often, and understaffed maintenance organizations cannot cope.

Water, milk, and other communal liquids are not advisable for consumption by visitors, but bottled water is available. Imported foodstuffs, clothing, and appliances are expensive because of heavy duties. Clifford Gardner, project manager for Marriott International's Omar Khayyam Hotel presently under construction in Cairo, gave us the following examples: one quart of peanut butter, $8; one can of beans, $3; one candy bar, $.80; one can of bacon, $6; one pair of sunglasses, $25; one pack of Western cigarettes, $2; one American newspaper, three weeks old, $3.

On the other hand, Mr. Gardner told us, there are plenty of good domestic foodstuffs and other products which are inexpensive: a fresh egg, $.03; a head of lettuce, $.06; a pound of peas, beans, rice, apples, oranges, etc., $.09. The same relative low costs are found for local meats, fish, and personal items such as clothing. Fruits and vegetables are fresh and abundant because the Nile Delta produces two or three crops per year. With proper sterilization and cooking, a visitor can eat well in Egypt on a modest budget.

There are endemic infectious diseases in Egypt of which the traveler must beware. Most common are viral and bacillary dysentery. A few American friends we met in Cairo were afflicted and suffered severely. However, there are a surprising number of English-speaking Egyptian doctors who were educated in the United States or in England, and the American Embassy furnishes a list. We remained free from infection because we took a preventive antibiotic, tetracycline, each day of our trip.

The climate is warm and arid, 40°F to 90°F in Cairo, 70°F to 125°F in Aswan. During our two weeks in Egypt we experienced an uncommon hot spell for early June. As obtained from *The Egyptian Gazette*, minimum and maximum temperatures from May 29 to June 7 in Fahrenheit were as follows:

	Alexandria	Cairo	Aswan
May 29	72–84	79–100	82–113
May 30	64–97	70–102	84–111
May 31	97	86–113	82–113
June 1	70–88	73–102	117
June 2	68–88	72–100	84–115
June 3	63–88	66–97	84–109
June 4	66–104	73–104	81–109
June 5	77–95	84–109	84–115
June 6	73	75–88	84–117
June 7	68–81	66–88	84–104

Egyptians, like most Arabs, are religious people, especially the Moslems, and they have strict rules of behavior. They generally frown upon drinking, although most large cities have a section of nightclubs. They do not like kissing, hugging, or even holding hands in public with the opposite sex; cursing; women smoking; or men with long hair. There is little crime, even in Cairo, perhaps because violators are dealt with swiftly and harshly. An eye for an eye still is practiced here.

A population of varied ethnic strains and races has existed harmoniously in Egypt for centuries. There is no discrimination and mixed marriages go unnoticed. There are still definite class stratifications, however; and although through Mme. Sadat's leadership a positive impact has been made on the issue of equal rights for women, Egypt still is decades behind the progress of the West.

Despite her problems, many of which we share, Egypt looks to the future uplifted by its proud past. It is a country with an irresistible magnetism in its history, its weather, its scenery, and its people. The beginnings of civilization are here, providing an experience that is both humbling and spiritual. Monumental structures inspired by an intensity of dedication perhaps never since equalled and testifying to the astounding industry and activity of the people. Religious precepts which provided sacerdotal practices from which later religions evolved. An excellence of art, agriculture and the sciences which flourished thirty-five hundred years ago. The adoption of a calendar and a written language two thousand years before other civilizations. Scholarly inquiries into philosophical questions of the mind and the universe. Extraordinary organization into diverse, but integrated, bureaucratic functions born of a sense of national unity and direction. A system of jurisprudence that laid the foundation for all bodies of law to follow. The incredible span of twenty centuries of almost continuous nationhood, rarely disturbed by outside incursions. An understanding of the environment and a respect for the ecological balance provided by the Nile. An orderly, sophisticated lifestyle that had purpose and meaning.

Ancient Egypt was the mother-lode of civilization. That influence, that tradition, that fabric of its remarkable people, still exist today. Given the days of peace and tranquillity she longs for, Egypt may once again reflect her ancient image deep and clear along the Nile.

Along the Nile at Aswan.

Bibliography

Aldred, Cyril. *Akhenaten: Pharaoh of Egypt.* London: Sphere Books Ltd., 1972.

Bonheur, Gaston. *Thebes of the Hundred Gates.* Cairo: Ministry of Culture, 1975.

Breasted, James Henry. *A History of Egypt.* Second Edition. New York: Charles Scribner's Sons, 1912.

Budge, E. A. Wallis, trans. *The Book of the Dead.* Secaucus, New Jersey: University Books, Inc., 1960.

Carter, Howard. *The Tomb of Tutankhamen.* New York: Excalibur Books, E. P. Dutton, 1972.

Casson, Lionel, and the editors of Time-Life Books. *Ancient Egypt.* New York: Time, Inc., 1965.

Doss, Latif and Besada, Asham. *The Story of Abu Simbel.* London: Longman Group Ltd., 1973.

Gilbert, Katharine Stoddert, with Holt, Joan K., and Hudson, Sara, eds. *Treasures of Tutankhamun.* New York: Metropolitan Museum of Art, 1976.

Hayes, William C. *The Scepter of Egypt.* New York: The Metropolitan Museum of Art, 1959.

Kamil, Jill. *Luxor, A Guide to Ancient Thebes,* Second Edition. London and New York: Longman Group Ltd., 1976.

Leacroft, Helen and Richard. *The Buildings of Ancient Egypt.* Leicester, England: Brockhampton Press; Reading, Massachusetts USA: Young Scott Books, 1969.

Riesterer, Peter. *Egyptian Museum Cairo.* Bern, Switzerland: Kummerly and Frey, 1975.

Index

Photo pages are indicated in **bold face** type

Abdine Palace, **viii**, 64–**65**, 130
Abu el Hagag (Mosque), 111
Abu Simbel, 54, 56, 89–95 (**88, 91, 94**) *See also* Color Plate Section II.
Abydos, 29, 54
Temple of, 56
After life, belief in, 16–17, 29–32, 38, 99. *See also* Religion.
Agilkia, 98, 100, **102**, 103, 105
Agriculture, 13, 16, 26, 32, 34, 38, 134
Akhenaten, 46–50, 51, 70, 74, 111, 114, 115, 118, 121, 124, 125
Akhetaten (Tel el-Amarna), 47, 51, 52, 115
Alabaster Mask, 8
Aldred, Cyril, 46
Alexander the Great, 21, 99, 111
Alexandria, 99
Amenophis I , 39, 115, 118, 121
Amenophis II, 43, 124
Amenophis III, 43–46, 51, 54, 74, 109, 111, 115, 118, 119
Amenophis IV (Akhenaten), 46–50
Ammenemes, The, 27–28, 32
Ammenemes III, 34
Amosis I, 36, 37, 39, 107

Amun, 15, 16, 29, 40, 42, 43, 44, 47, 48, 51, 53, 70, 90, 98, 99, 107, 108, 109, 111, 118
Ankhesenamun (Ankhesenpaten), 6, 50, 51, 52
Anubis, God, 5, 15, 69, 120. *See also* Color Plate Section I.
Aphrodite, 99
Art, Amarna, 54, 70, 74
Art and Architecture, 44, 53–54, 70, 74, 77, 80, 98, 99, 107, 111, 115, 118, 120
Artists and craftsmen, 56, 70, 74, 76
Arts and crafts, 33, 35, 82
Asia, 51, 54, 59
Aswan, 13, 18, 89, 92, 97–105, **136**
Aswan Dam, 93, 98, 100
Aten, 47–50, 51, 52, 74
Atum, (sun-god) (Re, Amun, Aten), 14, 15, 47–50, 51, 52
Atwa, Fouad, **101**, 104
Aurora (and Memnon), 120
Avaris, 37, 54
Avenue of the Pharaohs, 111, **117**
Ay, 51, 52, 124

El-Bagouri, Ahmad, 76
Barakat, Dr. Abo Eleyon, 119

Basta, Mounir, 80, **81**
Bastet, Goddess, 7
Bedouins, 26, 75, 82–84, 90
Belly dancing, 83, 87
Belzoni, Giovanni Battista,
    124
Bes, 15
Beverages, 76, 82, 97–98
Bird in Nest, 7, 63, 66, 69. *See*
    also Color Plate Section I
Boehm, Edward Marshall, 1
Book of the Dead, 30–32, 38,
    108
Breasted, James Henry,
    48–50, 52
Building and construction,
    ancient, 16, 17, 19, 23–25,
    26, 34, 38, 40, 44, 53–54,
    55–56, 120
    modern, 78
Burial grounds. *See* Tombs.
Buto, 15, 22

Caesar, Julius, 99
Cairo, **60**, 61–87, 107,
    130–131, 132, 133
    bazaars, 74
    climate, 62, 134–135
    population, 62, 78
Cairo Airport, 61
Cairo Museum, 4, 9, **57**, 64,
    68–74 (**71–73**), 76, **79**, 80,
    85, 130. *See also* Color
    Plate Section II.
Carnarvon, Lord, 124–127
Carter, Howard, 6, 69, 123,
    124–127, 129
Cartouche, 6
Ceremonial Chair Panel, 8
Ceremonies, religious, 109
Cheetah Head, 5, 69

Child King, bust of, 7–8. *See*
    also Color Plate Section
    I.
Christianity and Christians,
    49, 79–80, 99, 107, 111,
    123
Cleopatra VII, 99
Climate, 13, 19, 95, 123,
    134–135
Colossi, 44, 54, 56, 89–92,
    109, 111, 119
Commerce, 16, 22, 26, 34, 38,
    44, 56, 58
Constantine, Emperor, 80, 99
Coptic Museum, 80, **81**
Copts, 80

Dams, 92–93, 98, 100, **101**,
    103–104
Dashur, 33
Davis, Theodore, 124, 125
Deir el-Bahri, 41, 109, 119,
    120–**122**
Delta, 12, 13, 22, 43, 55, 56,
    58
Dionysius, 99
Diseases, travelers', 134
Djoser, 23
Doctors and medical
    assistance, 134
Dynasties,
    First and Second, 22
    Third, 23
    Fourth, 23, 25
    Fifth, 25
    Sixth, 25–6
    Seventh-Eleventh, 27
    Twelfth, 32
    Thirteenth, 34–35
    Fourteenth-Seventeenth,
    35

Eighteenth, 36
Nineteenth, 53

Early Dynastic Period, 22
Egypt, ancient,
  365-day calendar, 11, 22,
    135
  and its people, 12, 18, 19
  cultural changes in, 44
  decentralization of
    government, 25, 26, 27,
    37
  geography, 11–12
  historical calendar, 21, 22
  historical review, 21–59
  immigration, 56
  irrigation and canals, 13,
    22, 32–33
  maritime fleet, 16
  natural materials,
    importation of, 16, 26,
    40
  natural phenomena as
    gods, 14
  natural resources, 13
  political and social
    structure, 16
  social classes, 29
  weakening of the empire,
    43, 50, 56, 58–59
Eid, Yehia M., 119, 121, 123,
  127, 129
Eilts, Herman, U. S.
  Ambassador, 84, 85
Ennead, divine, 14–15
Ethiopians, 21, 98

Fahmy, Ismail, Egyptian
  Foreign Minister, 4
Faience Cup, 6, 69, 125. *See
  also* Color Plate Section

I.
Falcon Emblems, 7, 69
Feluccas, 110
First Intermediate Period,
  27–28
Flooding and its control, 92,
  93
Foods and restaurants, 63,
  76, 79, 84, 87, 97, 134
Ford, President Gerald R., 76

El-Gabry, Mondey S., 74–76
  (**75**), 79, 81–84
Galabiyas, 74
Gem-Aton, 48
Ghorbal, Ambassador Ashraf
  A., xii, 2, 4, 63
  and Mrs. Ghorbal, 3, 4, **9**,
    62–63, **131**, 133
  wedding of daughter
    Nahed, 4, 85–87 (**86**). *See
    also* Color Plate Section
    II.
Gizeh, 17, 18, 24, 64, 79, 114
Gods, early Egyptian, 14–16
Gold and precious materials,
  26, 54, 69, 108, 111, 126
Golden Throne Panel, 6
Greece, 59, 98, 99

Hapiru, 39, 46
Hapy, 16
Harpoonist, 8
Hashish, 83
Hassan, Dr. Ali, 68, 80, 97,
  109
Hathor (Sacred Cowhead) 5,
  90, 99, **113**, 120
Hatshepsut, **20**, 40–42, 109,
  115, 118, 119, 120–122,
  124

Queen Hatshepsut's
    Temple, *See* Deir el-
    Bahri.
Heh (god of eternity), 8
Heliopolis, 43, 48, 54, 62
Heracleopolis, 27, 56
Hermopolis, 48
Hermothis, 48
Hieroglyphic writing, 11, 22,
    99
High Dam, 92–93, 98, 100,
    101, 103–104
Hittites, 39, 46, 50, 51, 54, 55,
    56, 58
Horemheb, 51, 52–53, 118,
    124
Horus (falcon god), 6, 7, 14,
    15, 17, 22, 25, 27, 69, 99
Hotels and accommodations,
    62, 97, 110, **132**, 134
Housing, modern, 62
Hoving, Thomas, 76, 85
Hydroelectric power, 92, 103
Hyksos, 35–36, 37, 38, 39
Hypostyled hall design, 111,
    115

Ibis, 7
Imhotep, 23
Ineni, 40, 41
Inyotef family, 27
Iranians, 39
Isis (goddess of mother-
    hood), 15, 16, 90, 99, 100,
    105
Islam, 76–77, 80
Ivory Chest Lid, 6

Jewelry, 33, 79

"Ka" and "Ba," 17, 108

Kadesh, 39
Karnak, 40, 41, 43, 108, 109
    Great colonnaded hall,
        53–54, 55
    Temples, **10**, 44, 51, 52, **57**,
        106, 111, 114, **117**
Keb (earth god), 14–15
Khafre, 24
Khons, 16, 44, 118
Khufu (Cheops), 24
Kissinger, Dr. Henry A., 4,
    76
Kurna temple, 54, 55
Kush, 39, 54, 89

Lake Nasser, 90, 93, **101**, 105
Laws, 38, 40, 53, 136
Lepsius, Karl Richard, 124
Libyans, 54, 55, 58, 59
Literature, 33
Loret, Victor, 124
Lotus, 7, 22
Lower Egypt, 5, 22
Luxor, 44, 107–113
Luxor Museum, 9, 113
Luxor Temple, 44, **45**, 56,
    110–113 (**112**), **116**. *See
    also* Color Plate Section
    II.

Maat, 16
El-Malah, Madelaine Yassa,
    113
Manetho, 21
Marriage practices, 40, 43, 58
Mask of Tutankhamun, 5, **9**,
    15. *See also* Color Plate
    Section I.
Mastabas, 23, 38, 108
Medinet Habu, 121
Mediterranean Sea, 12, 13,

14, 26
Memnon, 111, 119–120
Memphis, 22, 23, 27, 35, 36, 43, 48, 54, 55, 56, 89
Menes, King, 22, 89
Menkaure, 24
Mentuhotpe, 27
Mentukerkhepeshef, 124
Merneptah, 58
Metals, use of, 35
Metropolitan Museum of Art, The, 4, 76, 85
Middle Kingdom, 29–34, 107, 115
Military activities, 26, 35, 36, 37, 42, 46, 51, 52, 54, 55, 56, 58, 89
Mines and quarries, 18, 22, 24, 103–104
Ministry of Culture, 61
Mitannis, 39
Mohammed, 77, 99
Mohssen, Mohammed, 68
Mokhtar, Dr. Mohammed Gamal El-Din, 63, 76, **77**, 78, 80, 97, 110, 129, 130
Mortuary practices, 16, 17, 29–30, 38
Mulla, Abd Al, 95
Museum of Islamic Art, 76
Music, 35, 83, 87, 110, 114
Mut, 16, 44, 90, 111, 118

Napoleon, 123
Nasser, President Gamal Abdel, 92
National Gallery, Washington, D. C., 1, 3, 4, 76, 85, 129
Natural resources in Egypt today, 133

El-Nawawe, Dr. Ibrahim, 3, 76
Necropolis, 119
Nefertari, 89–91
Nefertiti, 47, 49, 50, 51
Neith, 16
Nekhbet, 15, 22
Nephthys (goddess of women), 15, 16
New Kingdom, 36–58, 107, 108, 114, 121
Night clubs and entertainment, 81, 83
Nile River, 12–13, 14, 16, 17, **18**, 19, 62, 92, 93, 103, 105, 133, 134, **136**
Nixon, President Richard M., 4, 75
Nobles (nomarchs), 26, 27
and growth of middle class, 29
conflicts with pharaohs, 47, 48
power of, 27–28
Nu (god of darkness and chaos), 14, 15
Nubia, 12, 16, 26, 32, 34, 37, 39, 40, 43, 51, 54, 56, 59, 89
monuments of, 89–95
Nut (sky goddess), 14–15

Obelisks, 8, 40, 41, 43, 44, 56, 109, 111, 115, **117**
Old Kingdom, 23–26, 104, 107
Organization of Egyptian Antiquities, 4, 9, 10, 63, 76, 77, 78, 84, 130
Orontes River, 39
Osiris, 5, 7, 17, 29, 30, 31, 38,

48, 70, 90, 99, 118
    death of, 15

Palestine, 39, 42, 50, 54
Papyrus, 16, 22
"Papyrus of Ani," 30
Peace treaties, 55, 56
Pepi I, 26
Pepi II, 26
Peregrine Falcon, Boehm, 66
Perfume Bottles, 7. *See also*
    Color Plate Section I.
Persians, 21, 99
Petrie, Flinders, 124
Pharaohs,
    power and influence, 23,
        28, 108–109
    relationship to the gods,
        16, 23, 25, 70
Philae Island and Temples,
    92, 93, **96**, 97–105 (**101,
    102**)
Pococke, Norden and Bruce,
    123
Predynastic Age, 11, 22
Priests and administrators,
    16, 29, 58, 59, 74, 107
    conflict with pharaohs, 47,
        48
    growth of power, 25, 30,
        37–38
Psamtik I, 59
Psamtik II, 115
Ptah, 16, 90
Ptolemaic Period,
    (Ptolemies), 21, 99, 118
Ptolemy I, 99
Ptolemy IV, 115
Ptolemy XV Caesarion, 99
Punt, 120

Pylons, 53, 56, **96**, 109, 111,
    112
    at Karnak Temple, 115, 118
Pyramids, 23–25, 33, 38, 79,
    103, 108

Quarries, 18, 103–104

El-Rady, Ahmed Abd, **10, 45,**
    109–111, 114, 119, 129
Ramaden, 78
Rameses I, 53, 115, 124
Rameses II, **20,** 33, 53, 54–56,
    57, 58, 88–91, 95, 111,
    112, 115, 121, 124
Rameses III, 59, 115, 118, 121
Rameses VI, 122, 124, 125, 129
Ramesseum, 108, 109, 121
Ramessides, 53–59, 118, 121
Re, cult of, 25, 29
Red Sea, 16, 32, 54
Re-Harakhty, 15, 90
Religion, 38, 46–50, 51, 55,
    99, 135
    Christian (Christians), 49,
        79–80, 99, 107, 111, 123
    Coptic, 79–80
    Hebrew, 49
    Islam (Moslems), 76–77,
        99, 107, 111, 135
    Rituals, religious, 109
    Rome and Roman Empire,
        59, 80, 98, 99, 119–120

Sacred Cowhead, *See Hathor.*
El-Sadat, President Anwar, 4,
    61, 63, 66, 77, 133
El-Sadat, Mme. Anwar
    (Jehan), **viii,** 61, 64–68

(**65, 67**), 85, **86**, 130–**131**, 135

Sadat Center for Man's Civilization, 78

Sahara Desert, 13, 17, 61, 121

El-Sawi, Abd El-Monem, 77–78, 133

Sayed, Fathy, 61, 63, 68, 74, 79, 89, 130

Scarab, 6, 14, 38

Scarab Paperweight, Boehm, **39**

Sciences, development of, 22, 33

Scribes, 16, 23, 38

Second Intermediate Period, 35–36

Selket, Goddess, 7, 16. *See also* Color Plate Section I.

Semenkhkare, 50, 51, 74

Semites, 39

Senmut, 41, 120

Serapis, 99

Sesostris I, 32, 115

Sesostris II, 32, 56

Sesostris III, 33

Seth, 15, 17

Seti I, 53–55, 70, 115, 118, 121, 124, 129

Seti II, 115

Shawabty Figure, 8, 70, **71**

Sheshonk I, 59, 115

Shopping, **60**, 95, 110

Shoukry, Yeha, 104

Shu (god of atmosphere), 14

Siam, Abdin, 98, 99, **101**, 104

Slaves, 56, 108, 111

Smithsonian Institute, 100

Sneferu, 23

Sobek, 15

Social mores, 135

Soldiers, mercenary, 56, 58

Soptah, 124

"Sound and Light" presentations, 114

Sphinx, 18, 115, 118

Standard of living, modern, 134

Statuary, 44, 55, 56, 89–92, 118, 119–120. *See also* Colossi.

Sudan, 89, 92, 93, 105

Suez Canal, 133

Sun-god, 14, 15, 17

Syria (Syrians), 21, 37, 39, 42, 50, 54

Taharqa, 98, 115

Tanis, 56

Tanite-Amonites, 21

Taxes and treasury, 38, 59, 107

Tefnut (ocean god), 14

Tel el-Amarna (Akhetaten), 47, 51, 52, 74, 111, 124

Temperatures, 95, 123, 134–135

Temples and monuments, 33, 38, 40, 41, 42, 44, 47, 48, 53–54, 58, 59, 98, 107, 108

built by Rameses II, 55–56, 89–92

mortuary temples, 108–109, 119, 120–121

natural preservation of, 90, 92

relocation of, 92–95, 100–105

restoration of, 52–53, 92–93, 100–103, 111

Luxor, 110–113
  Karnak, 114–115, 118
    See also Building and
    construction.
Teti II, 26, 56
Thebes, 27, 29, 35, 38, 40, 41,
    42, 44, 47, 48, 51, 54, 55,
    74, 89, 107–108, 111. *See
    also* Luxor.
Thoth, 7
Thua, 124
Thutmosis I, 39, 40, 115, 124
Thutmosis II, 40, 115, 118,
    120, 121
Thutmosis III, 40, 43, 46, 55,
    56, 115, 118, 120, 121
Thutmosis IV, 43, 124
Tigris-Euphrates, civilization
    of, 12
  expansion to, 39
Tiye, Queen, **20**, 44–46, 47,
    51, 74, 111, 119
Tomb dwellers, 123
Tomb Guardians, 7, 69, **71**.
    See also Color Plate
    Section I.
Tomb robbing, 108, 121, 123,
    125
Tombs, 17, 18, 24–25, 27, 38,
    108, 121–**122**
  excavations of, 124–125
Tourism, 95, 133
Transportation and traffic,
    62, 95, 98, **105**, 110, 119,
    134
Tutankhamun,
  as king, 50–52, 74, 111
  death of, 52
  discovery of his tomb, 52,
    125–127

effect on people today, 2–3
  his tomb and its contents,
    69–70, **122**, 126–129,
    (128)
  historical importance, 52
  See also Color Plate Section
    II.
Tutankhamun collection,
  at the Cairo Museum,
    68–74
  technical challenge of re-
    creating, 8
  U. S. exhibition, 1, 3, 4, 68,
    69, 84–85, 130

UNESCO, 92, 93, 100
Upper Egypt, 5, 7, 22
Ushebtis (shawabtys, ushab-
    tis), 38
Utility service in Egypt
    today, 134

Valley of the Kings, 3, 6, 41,
    52, 54, 108, 109, 119–129.
    See also Color Plate Sec-
    tion II.
Valley of the Queens, 121
Votive Shield, 8

Warfare and armaments, 35,
    36, 37, 42, 46, 51, 52, 54,
    55
Wawat, 89
Women, role of, 65–66, 135

Yousuf, Abd El-Rauf Ali, 77
Yua, 124

Zeus, 99